Facing the Future

LEADERSHIP'S ROLE • VALUE/RETURN ON INVESTMENT (ROI) • RESPONSIVENESS

GOVERNANCE • REVENUE SOURCES • TECHNOLOGY USAGE • CHANGE LOOPS

GENERATIONAL ISSUES • WORKFORCE • OUTSOURCING AND CO-SOURCING • COMPETITION

AND ALLIANCES • CONSOLIDATION AND MERGERS • GLOBALIZATION • IMAGE BUILDING

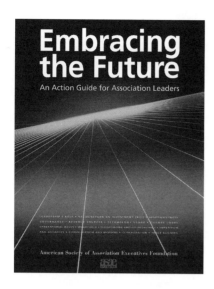

Embracing the Future

An Action Guide for Association Leaders

American Society of Association Executives Foundation

Coming Soon from the ASAE Foundation...

Look for *Embracing the Future: An Action Guide for Association Leaders,* a companion guide to *Facing the Future: A Report on the Major Trends and Issues Affecting Associations.*

Embracing the Future uses the important information gathered in *Facing the Future* as a launching pad to help you and your volunteer leaders and staff prepare for the future. This "futures toolkit" for associations is an essential step-by-step guide on how to lead your association to a successful future.

Facing the Future

A Report on the Major Trends and Issues Affecting Associations

Rhea L. Blanken and Allen Liff

asae | american society of
association executives

FOUNDATION

asae | american society of
association executives

American Society of Association Executives
1575 I Street, NW
Washington, DC 20005
Phone: (202) 626-2723
Fax: (202) 408-9634
E-mail: books@asaenet.org

George Moffat, Publisher
Linda Munday, Director of Book Publishing
Anna Nunan, Book Acquisitions Coordinator
Zachary Dorsey, Production Coordinator
Cover and interior design by Troy Scott Parker, Cimarron Design

Library of Congress Cataloging-in-Publication Data

Facing the future : a report on the major trends and issues affecting
    associations / ASAE Foundation.
        p.   cm.
    Includes bibliographical references (p.).
    ISBN 0-88034-150-5
    1. Trade and professional associations—United States—Management.
2. Trade and professional associations—United States—Management—
Problems, exercises, etc. I. American Society of Association Executives
Foundation.
HD2425.F3   1999
060'.68—dc21   98-54235
                                                              CIP

Printed in the United States of America.

This book is available at a special discount when ordered in bulk quantities. For information, contact the ASAE Member Service Center at (202) 371-0940. A complete catalog of titles is available on the ASAE home page at http://www.asaenet.org.

Contents

Foreword

Our careers as successful association executives will be enhanced by integrating this report into our processes, both internally within our staffs and externally throughout the association leadership structure. With this report, the American Society of Association Executives Foundation provides solid research on emerging trends affecting our collective futures. These trends mean different things to each of us and our associations. They influence our individual careers, our associations' future, and the future of our associations' members. These trends provide the framework for constructing a purposeful path.

The thought-provoking realities of this report urge us, as individuals and as association leaders, to have the courage to scan the horizon and boldly step forward based on our assessment of what these trends may mean. It's not enough to simply acknowledge that these trends are realistic. Nor is it appropriate to look at these trends as independent entities. They are interrelated, with different trends being emphasized with the different issues at stake. It is their collective reality that creates the synergy for a meaningful direction.

This report invites, even demands, an analysis of options. It is a means toward negotiating our tomorrows. It is a powerful, hands-on tool that can serve as a compass to help us plan for a successful future.

— John J. Prast, CAE
Executive Vice President
Million Dollar Round Table, Park Ridge, Ill.
Chair of the ASAE and ASAE Foundation Environmental Scan
Task Force

Preface

Your view of the future shapes your actions today,
and your actions today shape your future.
– DANIEL BURRUS, TECHNOLOGY FORECASTER AND FUTURIST

OVER THE PAST SEVERAL YEARS, executives have learned that today's associations face severe and immediate challenges that will impact their future success and viability. To address this concern, the American Society of Association Executives (ASAE) Foundation teamed with ASAE to conduct a comprehensive environmental scan of the association community. The Foundation is using the environmental scan to search for "road signs" about how the world is changing and how these changes are likely to affect associations.

Scanning the association environment is important to the Foundation for many reasons. Most important, doing so allows the Foundation to create and provide association executives with the tools to uncover new ways to manage change and prepare proactively for future challenges.

More than 2,500 chief executive officer members from small, medium, and large trade and professional organizations; convention and visitors bureaus; and the hospitality industry were surveyed for this report. The report's methodology also involved convening nine trend-analysis panels of executives and consultants in Washington, D.C.; Chicago; and Los Angeles; and conducting external interviews with experts in the for-profit sector.

The study uncovered 14 trends executives are addressing simultaneously, four compelling reasons why associations will thrive, the new rules of planning, and the characteristics associations will need to confront as they reshape themselves in the future. This report discusses these trends and issues in detail. It is a valuable resource that association executives can use when planning with their boards and staff.

– Thomas C. Dolan, Ph.D., FACHE, CAE
   President and Chief Executive Officer
   American College of Healthcare Executives, Chicago
   Past Chair of the ASAE and ASAE Foundation Environmental
     Scan Task Force

Acknowledgments

THIS REPORT is made possible through the hard work and dedication of many individuals. The American Society of Association Executives (ASAE) and the ASAE Foundation extend their thanks to Rhea L. Blanken of Results Technology, Inc., Bethesda, Md., and Allen Liff, Ronin Marketing, Washington, D.C., independent consultants who were commissioned by the Foundation to produce this report.

ASAE and the ASAE Foundation also thank the members of the 1998 ASAE and ASAE Foundation Environmental Scan Task Force for contributing their time and expertise:

Thomas C. Dolan, Ph.D., FACHE, CAE (Past-Chairman), president and chief executive officer of the American College of Healthcare Executives, Chicago

Sherry Keramidas, Ph.D., CAE, executive director, Regulatory Affairs Professionals Society, Rockville, Md.

Gary A. LaBranche, CAE, vice president, professional development, American Society of Association Executives, Washington, D.C.

Janet G. McCallen, CAE, executive director, International Association for Financial Planning, Atlanta, Ga.

Paul D. Meyer, LUTCF, CAE, vice president of executive management, American Society of Association Executives, Washington, D.C.

Ronald S. Moen, executive director, American Association of Orthodontists, St. Louis, Mo.

George E. Moffat, vice president of communications, American Society of Association Executives, Washington, D.C.

Elissa M. Myers, president, Electronic Retailing Association, Washington, D.C.

John J. Prast, CAE (Chairman), executive vice president, Million Dollar Round Table, Park Ridge, Ill.

Colin C. Rorrie, Jr., Ph.D., CAE, executive director, American College of Emergency Physicians, Irving, Texas

Sarah J. Sanford, chief executive officer, American Association of Critical-Care Nurses, Aliso Viejo, Calif.

Peg Scherbarth, regional sales director of sales, Walt Disney Attractions Inc., Washington, D.C.

Eve Shepard, director, information central, American Society of
    Association Executives, Washington, D.C.
John A. Tuccillo, Ph.D., CAE, president, John Tuccillo Associates,
    Arlington, Va.

The ASAE Foundation staff liaisons were Marsha L. Rhea, CAE,
executive vice president and chief operating officer, and Michelle I.
Mason, associate manager for Foundation programs.
The following individuals graciously donated their time to be interviewed as part of the environmental scan process:

Nigel Burton, Microsoft Corp., Redmond, Wash.
David Coleman, Collaborative Strategies, San Francisco
Erin Hiraoka, Microsoft Corp., Redmond, Wash.
Kathy Krajewski, Krajewski & Associates, Rockville, Md.
Marcia Kuszmaul, Microsoft Corp., Redmond, Wash.

Also making important contributions to this report were the numerous
environmental scan panelists who helped to shape and crystallize the
information gathered for this report. These contributors are listed in
Appendix A.

Thanks also go to the following for contributing their time and expertise in reviewing the drafts of this report:

Henry L. Ernstthal, JD, CAE
Ernstthal and Associates
Washington, D.C.

Ann C. Kenworthy, CAE
Chesapeake Beach, Md.

Donald M. Norris, Ph.D.
Strategic Initiatives
Herndon, Va.

Introduction

Recognizing that current information about emerging trends is essential for discovering tomorrow's opportunities, boards and staff are devoting more time and research to environmental scanning—the systematic and continuous effort to search for important cues about how the world is changing and how they will affect an organization. While there is no one right way or approach, environmental scanning generally does the following:

- Examines a broad range of issues, including economic, global, political, technological, and social trends.

- Gathers information from a variety of sources, such as literature reviews, surveys, interviews with experts, focus groups, scan panels, and site visits.

- Involves leading-edge thinkers, both inside and outside the industry or profession being scanned.

- Encourages "outside of the box" thinking by studying trends and changes occurring in unrelated industries or professions.

The advantages of environmental scanning are compelling. It enables the association to be more nimble and avoid the costly mistakes associated with reacting too slowly to foreseeable events. It also helps organizations uncover ways to implement and manage change successfully.

Research conducted on behalf of the ASAE Foundation has identified the need for associations to conduct two types of environmental scanning activities. The first looks at the industry or profession being served and is an activity unique to each association. The second looks at the trends and changes affecting all associations; that is the focus of the ASAE Foundation's activities and this report.

1998 Environmental Scan

The ASAE Foundation has continually monitored the trends affecting associations since 1995. In that year, a survey sent to more than 300 ASAE members identified major trends affecting associations. In both 1995 and 1996, the ASAE Foundation convened trend analysis panels in Washington, D.C., and Atlanta, Georgia, to explore the implications of the information technology explosion. Additional trend analysis panels were convened in 1996 specifically to explore the association governance process.

The ASAE Foundation held its New Horizons Think Tank in 1997. This high-level forum brought together leaders from both inside and outside the association industry to explore new ideas and get beyond incremental thinking about the future. Also that year, seven "Focus Groups on the Future" were held to learn how association CEOs prepare for the future.

In 1998, ASAE and the ASAE Foundation teamed up to conduct the most extensive scanning effort to date. The 1998 Environmental Scan, which involved association executives from all over the country, occurred in three stages.

▶ **Stage 1: Identification of Macro Trends.** Coates & Jarratt, a think tank and policy research firm that specializes in the future, worked with the ASAE Foundation to identify the broad issues or "macro trends" related to demographics, society, global economics, information and technology, and government and regulations. (A summary of these macro trends appears in the next section.)

In addition, interviews were held with experts from Microsoft, Collaborative Strategies, and Krajewski & Associates specifically to assess technology's promise for associations.

▶ **Stage Two: Interpretation of Macro Trends.** Next, association executives interpreted these macro trends by identifying the specific trends and issues most relevant to the association community. Feedback was gathered from association executives via a trend analysis survey faxed to 2,000 CEOs, e-mail queries to members participating in ASAE's Executive Management and Microsoft listserves, and telephone interviews with CEOs whose associations are undergoing major changes.

▶ **Stage Three: Convening of Scan Panels.** To thoroughly explore these trends, a series of nine all-day scan panels took place. Six panels were held for association CEOs—two panels each in Washington, D.C., Chicago, and Los Angeles. The panels reflected the full diversity of ASAE's membership, with representatives from both trade and individual membership organizations (IMOs), as well as organizations ranging in staff size from 1 to 300 people. In addition, panels were held with executives representing convention and visitor bureaus, the hospitality industry, and association consultants.

This publication, *Facing the Future: A Report on the Major Trends and Issues Affecting Associations,* presents the results of those scan panels.

Summary of Macro Trends

Here are the macro trends identified by Coates & Jarratt during the first stage of the ASAE Foundation's 1998 Environmental Scan. These trends provided the foundation on which the other two stages are built.

Demographic Trends

TREND: The U.S. population is aging, and more of our elders will be over 75.

The United States is an aging nation. Its median age, which today is 33, will be 38 by 2020, with the population aging about 1 to 1.5 years in every 5 years. The trend toward a larger older population in the United States will be gradual until 2010. Then, between 2010 and 2030, the older population will grow by 73% as the first Baby Boomers turn 65, and the grandparent boom begins.

TREND: The entry of the Baby Boomers' children into school, and later into the workforce, is creating a new youth bulge in the population.

A much larger generation than the Baby Bust, the Baby Boomers' children (also known as the Echo generation) will be entering the workforce in large numbers in 2005. This will put an end to the relative scarcity of young people in the current workforce. Today, about 30% of the U.S. population are Baby Boomers, and 27% belong to the Baby Boom Echo.

TREND: Immigration and the growth of minorities drive toward a multi-racial, multi-ethnic society.

The United States is becoming a society of diverse racial and ethnic minorities. By 2020, the groups known as minorities today will represent 36% of all Americans. Higher birth rates among minorities and immigrants will cause these groups to grow faster. The future U.S. population will be composed of older white people and younger minorities.

TREND: The Baby Boomer generation is maturing, aging today's workforce.

The Baby Boomers, whose entry-level numbers kept the workforce young in the 1970s, now leads the middle-aging of that workforce into the 21st century. The median age of the workforce, which had dropped to 34.5 in 1979, will rise to 38.9 by 2000. The end of the 1990s will see the completion of a shift to a workforce and a society dominated by middle-aged Boomers. This means a more experienced, educated workforce, but at a higher cost in compensation and benefits.

Social Trends

TREND: Middle-class values become dominant in the United States.

As an educated, urban, prosperous society, at least 70% of the U.S. population now shares middle-class values. These values, which do not depend entirely on income, include:

- The questioning and rejection of arbitrary authority
- A focus on quality
- A growing ambivalence toward risk
- An increased passion for procedure

TREND: Distribution of income in the United States favors upper-income groups.

The GINI Index, which measures the distribution of income, shows that annual income in the United States has become more unevenly distributed each year since 1980.

TREND: The workforce is becoming more diverse.

By 2005, the U.S. workforce will be 73% white, 12% black, 11.2% Hispanic, and 4.3% Asian and other minorities.

White women will represent 33% of the workforce. Black women will increase their share to 6.3% and Hispanic women to 4.6%. In 1995, 12% of the employees in U.S. corporations were minorities, compared to 2% in 1966.

TREND: Nontraditional families proliferate.

A variety of nontraditional family forms are evolving in the United States. Shaped by economic and social changes, the emerging family types include:

- Boomerang families (adult children return home)
- Blended families (divorced parents remarry)
- Technologically created families (test-tube babies, use of fertility drugs, genetically matched adopted children, etc.)
- Gay families
- Temporary families (group living, often during a transitional life stage)
- Single-parent families (at least 10.5 million)

TREND: Distributed work—particularly computer-supported work—continues to expand.

Distributed work is being done at home and in cars, vans, planes, and hotels—anywhere someone can connect via an electronic network to the home office or to co-workers. The number of U.S. telecommuters has risen from 8.5 million in 1995 to about 11 million; nearly one out of three (31%) telecommuters use the Internet.

TREND: The contingent workforce is growing.

Fewer people now have permanent jobs, and fewer still expect to keep those jobs for most of their working lives. Using a broad definition of contingency, about 25% to 31% of the workforce are contingent—between 34 million and 42 million people. Since the mid-1980s, corporations have laid off more than 3.5 million workers.

How to Use This Report

This report is intended to *galvanize* the leadership of your association as they endeavor to meet the challenges of the future and to *facilitate* their discovery of emerging opportunities. The ASAE Foundation's ongoing research reaffirms the need for associations to reshape themselves to remain competitive and relevant to their members and the public. For many, radical shifts rather than incremental changes will be the organizational imperative.

The challenge facing every association is to uncover ways to implement and manage change successfully. More than ever, association boards and staff will have to anticipate the future and take action in the face of its uncertainties. These same issues and concerns are being addressed by the boards of corporations, institutions of higher education, and nonprofits. Every profession, business, or industry is affected.

As you read this report keep in mind that it serves two important functions:

▶ **Enables boards and staff to think and act strategically regarding their future.** When it comes to designing the 21st century association, there are few answers and proven techniques. The CEOs who participated in the environmental scan panels acknowledged they were heading into uncharted territory where in-depth information on many trends is not yet available. In the face of this uncertainty, they asked that ASAE provide thinking tools and an action guide that would engage their boards in asking the right questions about the future.

► **Facilitates leadership dialogues within your association.** To arrive at robust solutions for tomorrow, executives will need to facilitate dialogues both inside and outside the association. Internally, the chief staff executive must engage the entire board and staff in a dynamic and creative visioning process—there can be no one on the sidelines. External dialogue with other association and for-profit corporate leaders will expose the executive to new perspectives and form the basis for cooperative problem solving.

In both cases, you can use this report as a facilitation tool to ensure that everyone starts the creative visioning process with a shared understanding. All the participants will have the same information on hand and be able to use the same language to discuss the information.

Part I of this report provides, in a narrative style, an overview of the broad changes affecting all associations, highlights of the ASAE Foundation's 1998 Environmental Scan, and key implications for associations. This narrative is intended to help boards and staff see the "big picture" that arises from all the information contained in the scan. It also provides a background briefing on the depth and breadth of changes sweeping through the entire association community.

Part II provides more in-depth discussion about each of the 14 trends and five association characteristics that were uncovered during the environmental scan.

Facing the Future concludes with some additional information relevant to the process of envisioning the future. A bibliography and suggested reading list offer recommendations for learning more about specific trends or association characteristics. In the two appendices that follow, you'll find a list of all the association executives who participated in the environmental scan panels, as well as instructions for conducting a future scan dialogue session with your own board members and staff.

PART I

An Overview of the Changes

1

The Changing Face of Associations

A Historical Perspective

IF YOU TRACE the history of associations in America and examine their benefits to society, it becomes obvious that associations must make adjustments to remain relevant. Associations have accommodated an uncertain future before—they can do it again.

In 1743 the American Philosophical Society is founded in Philadelphia.

In 1768, 20 merchants establish the New York Chamber of Commerce.

By the 1870s, the United States has approximately 100 trade associations.

Between the start and end of World War I (1914–1920) the number of U.S. associations doubles to 2,000.

In 1920, American Trade Association Executives is founded (the predecessor of ASAE).

After World War II ends in 1945, volunteer efforts increase noticeably throughout society.

Satellite transmissions become commonplace during the 1970s.

Associations become business-like in the 1980s, focusing on the bottom line.

In 1995, 10% of associations have Web sites; two years later, 60% have them.

2005—What will associations look like?

The first transformation of associations actually occurred with the Puritan settlers of New England. They emphasized the value of the individual within the community—a direct break from the Western European guild model.

From its very beginning, America's diverse geography and ideological attitudes provided a rich environment for people to be part of a community while still maintaining their sense of individualism—that was also the focus for associations.

In 1830, in his book *Democracy in America*, the Frenchman Alexis de Tocqueville observed, "Americans of all ages, all stations of life, and all types of dispositions are forever forming associations." With well over 23,000 national associations in the United States today, we are still forming associations.

For more than 200 years, America has been populated by civic leagues, social brotherhoods, and federated groups representing both trade and professional interests. As these organizations continue to mature and provide more and more benefits, our society has continued to improve.

Over the years, the need for specialized education and information, research, and standardization has grown. Associations have delivered these and other services with increasing proficiency. In fact, the single most dominant activity associations perform for their members and the public is education.

Associations have amassed their own "Body of Knowledge"—unique and specialized technical information and leadership development. Association-related educational opportunities and information dissemination are available to today's members. But what will they need in the future?

In 1995, ASAE Foundation research concluded: "Associations must change the way they do business or they will not survive in the 21st century." It echoed Charles Darwin who wrote, more than a century earlier, "It is not the strongest of the species that survives, nor the most intelligent, but the one most responsive to change."

Now is the time to address change in your association.

An Inventory of Change

Following is an abbreviated inventory of eight critical changes sweeping through associations. Its purpose is to provide a sense of the *breadth* of changes affecting associations. This inventory is not meant to be an all-inclusive list but rather to illustrate additional changes not necessarily covered in the case studies that follow.

1. The Internet

The most powerful theme of this technology is its ability to increase inter-activity. Innovative uses by associations include:

▶ Creating an "online collaboratory" to foster continuous learning around a specific educational event.

▶ Providing interactive educational programming before, during, and after the annual meeting.

▶ Extending the excitement and information communicated during an association's legislative action conference. Using a digital camera, the association posts action shots of all major speakers on its Web site; speeches are audiotaped and available for downloading by nonattendees. Before the conference, the association also used the Internet to gain considerable input on pending legislation from members.

▶ Developing interactive databases accessible via the Internet. One association has designed a database to monitor technical issues and share solutions among its membership. Another is developing a database of information about the wants, needs, and preferences of its members and other industry stakeholders. The information from the state and national levels is integrated into one interactive database, leading to an unprecedented capability for knowledge sharing within the industry.

▶ Becoming familiar with meeting facilities by accessing online, virtual-reality tours of convention centers and hotels. Views of exhibit halls, seminar rooms, social galleries, and even diverse room set-ups are available at the touch of a button. This enables association executives to plan meetings and set up trade shows without ever leaving their offices.

▶ Sponsoring a virtual trade show for members that includes quick-time video, online registration, multi-lingual support, exhibition floor plans, and search engines.

▶ Offering distance education. When one association learned that 80% of its members already had computers in their businesses, it decided to focus on distance education via the Internet and interactive CD-ROMs to help members meet state mandates for continuing education. The flexibility of time is important for a membership whose work requires them to be on call 24 hours a day.

▶ Using telecommuting to cut costs for an educational organization. Breaking with tradition, education faculty live all over the country and communicate with one another by conference calls and e-mail. They fly to designated cities to conduct their short weekend courses based on a flexible schedule and hold their annual meeting aboard a cruise ship during the winter holidays.

▶ Using Web sites to deliver membership recruitment tracking information. Online, members can quickly track the progress of their referrals during member-get-a-member campaigns.

In addition to the power of its interactivity, the Internet promises to dramatically reduce publishing and communication costs. One association, for example, has already achieved cost reductions in three areas: telephone costs (down 27%), postage costs (down 44%), and publication costs (down 66%).

2. Shifts in Strategic Focus

Virtually every association, in response to rising member expectations, is becoming more focused, changing its revenue formulas, and making strategic shifts. For instance, the *ASAE Trend Analysis Survey* indicates that a majority of associations (82%) have initiated major new programs or services, and more than half (54%) have changed their membership structure (including online-only members, expanding international memberships, and creating "tiered" memberships to accommodate mergers). About one in three associations (32%) has narrowed its focus by dropping programs. Nearly half (46%) indicated a change in financial structure, such as unbundling services that were traditionally included in the dues and creating fee-based services.

More specifically, here are examples of what some associations are doing:

▶ Uncoupling the product and program development process from the governance process to speed the delivery of new benefits to members.

▶ Narrowing their focus so they can better concentrate on what they do best. Some organizations have:

    – Outsourced their product and fulfillment businesses.
    – Sold their product catalog business to a long-time competitor.

– Reduced staff by 40% by focusing solely on government relations.

– Partnered with educational institutions to provide educational programming. The association provides the faculty and content; the institution provides the venue, as well as all event-related logistics, promotions, and registrations.

▶ Shifting from mass marketing and segmentation to a one-to-one mass customization marketing effort. This enables them to tailor information-related products and services to individual member needs.

▶ Setting up regional councils, market segment "alliances," or other special structures to develop and deliver services to specific segments within their membership. In a few cases, trade associations have refocused their mission on a narrower, more strictly defined industry segment.

One trade association recently transformed its volunteer committee structure. Instead of forming around traditional interest areas, such as education, membership, and publications, committees now represent members by various sales volume (up to $1 million, $1 million to $5 million, $5 million to $10 million, and so forth). The association sees the potential for aligning staff by these same segments and having segment managers.

▶ Moving to fee-based services and greater accountability to members. Some organizations have:

– Developed a revenue system based on *à la carte* services. After paying initial dues, which include a periodical (via mail, fax, or e-mail), members purchase everything else for a separate fee.

– Developed fee-based services and activity-based accounting practices akin to how a law or consulting firm operates. Staff track their hours, which are then billable to the various product groups represented within the association. One organization tracks its staff-to-member interactions according to its annual selection of key issues and priorities in the industry.

– Based each member company's dues on manufacturing volume, with additional fee-for-services provided in specialized areas. For instance, members pay for what they use over a specified limit for product testing, claims, and legal services. Other services, crisis management consulting, and customized or on-site training are considered *à la carte* and priced separately.

3. Outsourcing/Co-sourcing

More and more associations are using outsourced or co-sourced partners, often in the areas of technology and meeting and conference management. Thanks to such an arrangement, one association serves 15,000 members with only two staff members.

According to Donald M. Norris, co-sourcing is a new breed of outsourcing that involves closer relationships between associations and vendors. In a co-sourcing arrangement, association staff maintain a function in-house while collaborating with a co-source partner to enhance the function.

4. Volunteer Management

A shift is occurring away from long-term, time-intensive volunteer commitments toward short-term, tightly focused volunteer opportunities. In one association, a special interest group has even set up a volunteer structure that intentionally turns over monthly. The new volunteer structure requires a time commitment of two to three months (to plan and host educational events) versus the traditional, one-year committee appointment. The short-term assignments have resulted in greater volunteer participation.

More and more association programs are being designed from the volunteers' perspective of time commitments and their desire for career development. Year-long membership campaigns are encouraging members to identify the specific months they will be participating from the menu of volunteer tasks available. The campaign goes on all year, but the volunteers rotate in and out based on their schedules.

5. Organizational Structure and Culture

ASAE's *1998 Foundation Trends Analysis Survey* revealed that nearly 60% of respondents reported a change in how staff was structured or human resources were managed. This included increases in the use of part-time employees.

Some associations are abandoning a traditional hierarchical staff arrangement and moving to a system of self-managed teams. One has organized its staff teams around four core business processes: business development, product development, production, and customer service and fulfillment. Another has opted to organize its staff according to functional groups, such as association management, operations and finance, and professional affairs. One pioneering association has even eliminated job titles for staff. These shifts to team-based environments are accompanied by "cultural realignments," which can often lead to significant turnover of staff who are not comfortable working in a collaborative, nonhierarchical environment.

6. Governance

Two out of five respondents (41%) to the *1998 Foundation Trends Analysis Survey* said their associations had changed the governance structure, most often by reducing board size; changing board composition (including a shift from regional representation); eliminating standing committees in favor of ad hoc, project-based task forces; and lengthening board terms (for instance, going from one-year terms with complete board turnover each year to two-year, staggered terms).

Specific changes include:

▶ Using technology to speed and enhance the governance process. Online review of planning documents, agenda discussions, and increased communication between board meetings are becoming commonplace. One association set up a listserve just for board members; they use it to engage in electronic decision making, including debating motions, offering amendments, and calling for votes. Another association has conducted its strategic planning exercises online. The planning group posted its work on the Web, enabling all team members (and eventually the entire membership) to review the results.

▶ The emergence of for-profit associations. Some organizations are now being set up as for-profit entities and eschewing the traditional 501(c)(3) or (c)(6) formats.

7. Competition

In a survey conducted by the ASAE Foundation, three out of four respondents (76%) said their associations are facing more competition from more sources than ever before. Typically, that competition comes in the form of another association (83%), another service provider (58%), another publisher (17%), or a for-profit trade show (16%).

8. Partnerships

Associations are increasingly seeking out nontraditional partners. Examples include:

▶ Amazon.com, the virtual super-bookstore, is working with organizations to create online bookstores of interest to their constituencies. Through the Amazon Associates program, associations can customize book collections, publish reviews, and help readers purchase books on their Web sites through a link to Amazon.com. The bookstore fulfills the order, handles the cash processing, and issues a quarterly commission check (up to 15% of sales plus referral fees).

▶ An investment firm that offers a one-to-one customized financial program for associations now hosts an annual meeting for its association partners. The meeting offers membership marketing training to executives, as well as briefings on key trends.

▶ A medical association has entered into an agreement to lend its endorsement to vitamin supplements marketed by vitamin manufacturer Nature Made.

▶ Microsoft has built alliances with ASAE and the U.S. Chamber of Commerce to reach the small business market.

Case Studies: Associations in Transition

The five case studies that follow illustrate the *depth* and the inter-related complexity of the issues facing associations, as well as the dramatic responses that have occurred. The trends noted in the left column are summarized in the next chapter and examined in greater detail in Chapter 5.

Founded: 1973

Scope: State

Staff Size: 4

Membership:
300 healthcare agencies

Inter-related Trends:
- Revenue Sources
- Governance
- Leadership's Role
- Value/Return on Investment (ROI)
- Responsiveness

When this association was founded in the 1970s, its dues structure was based on assessing the number of visits or hours of service provided by the member agency. With the advent of managed care and changes in regulation, the industry underwent massive realignment. At that point the association faced several major challenges at once:

- New entrants into the field had different operating models. The traditional membership categories, based on visits/hours of service, excluded these new players. As a result, membership was out of alignment with the industry.
- Changes in the healthcare field meant that members and potential members were in need of new types of services.
- The antiquated bylaws hindered the association's ability to respond to rapid change.
- The association's culture was still dominated by the nucleus of founding members and therefore did not reflect the current or future direction of the industry.
- The association had only a rudimentary strategic plan.

In the face of these inter-related issues, the executive director concluded that a piecemeal approach would not work. A holistic solution was needed to address the dues structure, membership categories, and governance—all at the same time. The executive director led the board through a visioning process that:

- Eschewed any attempts at incremental solutions.
- Required the board to envision what the industry and association would be like 10 years out, then work backward from the future to redesign the association.
- Explored a number of future scenarios and possible solutions before coming up with the final solution.

As a result of this process, the association made three major changes:

- Completely overhauled the dues structure and membership categories.
- Rewrote the bylaws to enable responsiveness to the current industry environment.
- Shifted the board away from micromanagement to a strategic mindset. Board agendas have been deliberately crafted to support this culture shift. In addition, traditional standing committees are being eliminated in favor of flexible, ad hoc ways of organizing volunteers around specific issues or tasks.

The executive director says she's found few other associations pushing the envelope and, consequently, is "inventing as she goes along."

Founded: 1950s

Scope: State

Staff Size: 25

Membership:
1,000 businesses in the
construction industry

Inter-related Trends:
• Leadership's Role
• Workforce
• Responsiveness
• Generational Issues
• Governance
• Technology Usage
• Alliances

In 1991 this association was in the midst of a financial crisis so severe that it was on the verge of going "belly up." To make a fresh start, the association sought an executive director with a business background and no prior association experience.

Upon his arrival the new executive said, "You will lose the association if you don't change your ways." What followed can only be described as a massive overhaul of both culture and structure:

• The executive deliberately set out to build a staff culture organized around teams and knowledge sharing. That required replacing almost the entire staff and hiring people with no association experience and often no construction industry background.

• Staff are no longer organized according to departments. Instead, they mobilize in flexible, ad hoc ways around core service groups.

• The board culture shifted in response to the crisis facing the association. An influx of younger board members gave the association a new generation of leaders who were willing to take risks and pioneer new ways of doing business.

• The strategic planning process was totally revamped to enable true strategic thinking and continuity over multi-year spans. Current and incoming board members agree to support a planning model based on a four-year cycle so a consistent vision can be maintained over time. This is a deliberate attempt to avoid the annual shifts in strategic direction that used to occur with each incoming board president.

• The governance structure was streamlined by creating special interest groups called "councils" where like-minded members could coalesce around issues important to them. Most standing committees were eliminated.

The association is leveraging technology as an image-building tool. It is positioning the local construction industry as a leader based on the ability to use technology. The association is also showing members how to use technology as a strategic advantage in their businesses.

In addition, the statewide association is using the Internet to better communicate with other chapters and form alliances that bypass what is perceived as an unresponsive national headquarters. This reflects the "culture clash" between the state chapter and its national association, which is rooted in regional differences in the construction industry that are not adequately represented by the national staff and in the national headquarters' seeming inability to capitalize on the use of technology.

Founded: 1955

Scope: National

Staff Size: 5

Membership:
1,800+ cultural institutions
and 800+ associates

Inter-related Trends:
- Value/Return on Investment (ROI)
- Leadership's Role
- Responsiveness
- Workforce
- Technology Usage

This association's transformation was built upon the executive director's belief that "we must listen to the changing environment and be very flexible." In redesigning her association, she drew upon examples of relatedness found in nature. The intended outcome was the creation of a "self-organizing learning environment versus a command-and-control model."

The organization needed to expand services and staff competencies. However, simply hiring more staff to implement new programs and services was not the approach the executive director wanted to follow. The real need was not for *more* staff but the *right* staff with the skills and mindset that could fulfill the future needs and the expectations of the members.

To realize this vision, the executive director met with staff and described her new set of expectations. Staff were expected to share knowledge freely and work in teams so they could focus effectively on the needs of the membership. She asked them to re-align their focus from individual department responsibilities to participating in the overarching decisions being made for the entire organization.

This shift in the environment emphasized participatory behavior, staff responsiveness to one another, and the flexibility necessary to seize future opportunities. Staff were expected to focus on outcomes rather than tasks and to use technology to facilitate organization-wide collaboration. Two-thirds of the staff decided they could not fit into this new culture.

On a more positive note, the following developments have occurred:

- The executive director hired new staff who thrive in a participatory culture. (Note: The association outsources "testing" of job candidates to carefully match their personalities and talents with the organization's vision.)
- Job descriptions focus more on essential outcomes and less on task-oriented or departmental activities.
- Staff come together to create the association's programs in a truly collaborative spirit.
- An improved organizational infrastructure has resulted from a large investment in hardware and software.
- The new environment challenges staff to do whatever is necessary for the association's success.
- A sense has developed among staff that they "own" their job responsibilities and can contribute to increased revenues for the association.

Founded: 1986

Scope: National

Staff Size: In 20 months, increased from 19 to 35

Membership: 7,500+ individuals

Inter-related Trends:
- Leadership's Role
- Value/Return on Investment (ROI)
- Responsiveness
- Revenue Sources
- Globalization
- Competition
- Technology Usage

This scientific association has rolled out a new member service or product every four weeks for 14 months in a row. A few examples include:

- The number of workshop offerings has increased 50%.
- The traditional newsletter has grown into a newsmagazine, with immediate and significant revenue benefits to the organization.
- A new online career center quickly attracted many subscribers.
- The association's latest online exposition was a financial success.
- Its "Education Anytime" effort provides short, online learning courses available to members around the world: from their hotel rooms as they travel on business, back at their offices, or at home on weekends. Because the association can deliver educational programming anywhere in the world, it considers itself "boundaryless."
- The association has used the Internet to launch 10 discussion groups organized by geographic regions; 9 special topic discussion groups; and 18 ongoing, interactive focus groups.

All the association's online services and offerings are meeting or exceeding their budgeted expectations. These efforts have been so successful that they represent a financially competitive threat to a long-established, for-profit publisher that counts the association's members among its subscribers.

How did this association become such a prolific developer of new products and services? In 1995 the board created a "2020 Strategic Plan" that gave strategic direction to the staff. The executive director made sure the entire staff participated in designing the tactics to carry out the board's vision.

The first tactical plan resulted in a daunting challenge. It identified 99 audiences to be served, 62 services that needed to be created or improved to fulfill the expectations of their members and customers, and 70 different vehicles appropriate for their delivery.

To keep such a complex plan updated and vibrant, the staff have created what they refer to as a *living* plan. During monthly staff meetings they discuss what programs, products, and services to keep, enhance, sunset, or invent. Everyone on staff participates in these conversations. The association also empowers its staff by actively outsourcing noncore functions so they can devote their energy toward creating value for the membership.

Founded: 1987

Scope: National

Staff Size: 2 (with volunteer leaders doing the work of 5–7 staff from the field)

Membership:
2,000+ individuals

Inter-related Trends:
- Leadership's Role
- Governance
- Technology Usage
- Responsiveness
- Change Loops

Are "headquarters-less" associations possible? Do they represent the future of association management? Are volunteer boards capable of making swift decisions on an as-needed basis?

One sports-related foundation thinks so. In the beginning the founding members rented office space from another association and hired a full-time staff executive whose main responsibilities were to run the government relations program and go "on the road" to promote the organization's image to related state associations.

Rather than hire more staff, the volunteer leadership decided to run all organizational functions, except government relations and public relations, from their own offices. At the time, the president/CEO lived in Indiana, one vice president in Kansas, another in Colorado, and the treasurer in Georgia. The volunteer directors of Events & Conferences, Communications, Products, State Representatives, and Membership all lived in different states as well.

The national office in Washington, D.C., serves as the main focus for the group's lobbying efforts and for building relations with state-level aligned organizations. It's also a place were members can work when they come to visit their congressional representatives.

The president (now from Colorado) coordinates most governance activities via e-mail. The bylaws were designed to foster flexible processes that lead to quick decision making: Elected leaders can take up issues and make decisions via e-mail ballots anytime during the year. Decisions are made on an as-needed basis, and important issues are not left unresolved for months at a time or "held hostage" until the next board meeting.

CHAPTER

Looking into the Future

In MAY 1998, association CEOs had an unprecedented opportunity to meet and conduct a dialogue about the future. Six panels were held for association CEOs—two panels each in Washington, D.C., Chicago, and Los Angeles. The participants reflected the full diversity of ASAE's membership, with representatives from trade and individual membership organizations as well as organizations ranging in staff size from 1 to 300 people. In addition, panels were held with executives of convention and visitor bureaus, hospitality executives, and association consultants.

During every panel, regardless of location, the executives spoke eloquently and passionately about the magnitude and nature of change that is sweeping through the association community. This chapter summarizes their observations and conclusions about the future.

Do not underestimate the magnitude of change that is coming.

The panel participants were asked to think about the trends affecting their associations and envision plausible future scenarios resulting from those trends. As part of the exercise, the CEOs wrote "future headlines" describing the changes they believe would likely occur in the next three to five years.

The resulting headlines and scenarios reveal that CEOs are encountering profound changes in all aspects of how their associations do business. Consequently, they envision the need for major changes in their organizations—incremental changes or tweaking of existing processes will not suffice. As you'll see, the headlines highlight both the range and the magnitude of change that is occurring. This change encompasses an impressive spectrum of issues, including organization design, generational conflict, governance, technology, global issues—and much more. By all measures, an unprecedented degree of change is sweeping through the association community.

Here are some of the future headlines written during the panels:

First Day of Annual Meeting Scheduled for February 2 on Your PC

Xer Revolt Leads to Rash of New Specialty Associations

Telecommuting Results in 80% Office Vacancy

Association Offers Short-Term, ad hoc Memberships—Annual Dues Obsolete

Association Goes Virtual: Headquarters Building Sold for $10 Million

Pay-As-You-Need Schemes Emerge to Replace Traditional Dues

Face-to-Face Meetings Rebound as Dissatisfaction with Virtual Meetings Takes Hold

Internet Delivery Radically Lowers Costs

Technology Revolutionizes Governance Systems of Associations

Association's Cable TV Interactive Network Rated Top Member Benefit

Associations in Hand-to-Hand Combat with For-Profit Companies

Association Staff Consists of Contract Employees in 100 Key Cities

Size of Association Staffs Greatly Reduced by Technology

State and Local Chapters Revolt Against National Headquarters

Virtual Trade Show Revenues Exceed Those of Traditional Expos

Multi-Lingual Services Become the Norm

To gain additional perspective on why association executives believe major shifts or realignments are imminent, consider that they are facing change on four fronts:

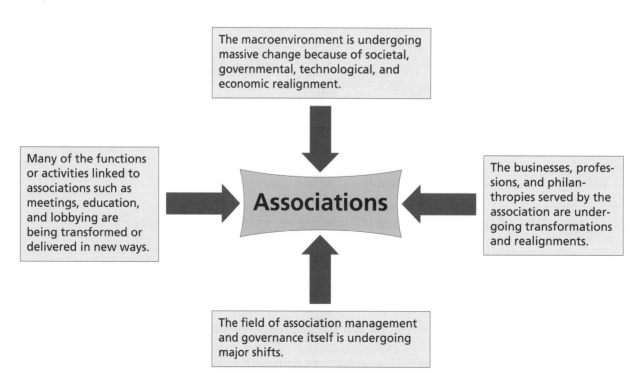

The macroenvironment is undergoing massive change because of societal, governmental, technological, and economic realignment.

Many of the functions or activities linked to associations such as meetings, education, and lobbying are being transformed or delivered in new ways.

Associations

The businesses, professions, and philanthropies served by the association are undergoing transformations and realignments.

The field of association management and governance itself is undergoing major shifts.

14 inter-related trends are driving this change.

In designing the environmental scan we hypothesized that each scan panel would be able to identify and prioritize a narrow list of three to five top trends affecting their associations. Instead, we learned that many changes are occurring simultaneously and their effects are inter-related. The intertwined complexity and multitude of change is clearly illustrated in the case studies included in Chapter 1.

In total, the participants identified 14 broad themes. Any of them might be viewed as a "trend," an "impact," or an "issue," depending on your association's perspective. While the scan panelists consistently referred to the same set of 14 themes, *how* those themes were referenced differed in the following ways:

- A *trend* has had no effect on the association yet but has clear implications for the near future.
- An *impact* means the effects are already playing out in the association.
- An *issue* has the potential for affecting the association in the future and should be monitored.

Note: For the purposes of this report, the term *trend* is used for consistency.

Every association is likely to be dealing with at least 4 or 5 of these trends at one time; some may deal with 10, 12, or even all 14. In other words, it is impossible and misleading to explore a single trend without considering how it interacts with the others—the boundaries between issues are blurring. For this reason, panelists noted that trying to prioritize trends seemed an arbitrary exercise. Examining the whole range of issues holistically was seen as a more powerful way to capture the complexity of the situation facing an association.

The 14 trends, which are discussed in depth in Chapter 5, are:

Leadership's Role—Adopting a new set of leadership characteristics will be the first step for association boards and staff as they move into the 21st century.

Value/Return on Investment (ROI)—Meeting rising member expectations and a greater demand for a return on the dues investment will drive the redesign of associations.

Responsiveness—Keeping up with external changes and responding rapidly to members' emerging needs will require associations to become "fast, fluid, and flexible."

Governance—The inability of current governance models (which are slow and cumbersome) to deal with an increasingly complex, fast-paced environment will require a cultural shift for most associations.

Revenue Sources—The need for new revenues will drive associations to become more innovative in seeking out new partners and nontraditional sources of income.

Technology Usage—The profound and beneficial effects of technology usage will be felt through its increasing capability to link people, build relationships, and foster communities.

Change Loops—Mastering the unplanned changes and unexpected consequences (i.e., "change loops") that do not fall neatly inside the time frame of the traditional planning calendar or scheduled board meetings will require a new mindset about the budget and planning process.

Generational Issues—The generational shifts among staff, board, and members (Matures born before 1946, Boomers born between 1946 and 1964, and Generation X born between 1965 and 1985) will fundamentally alter the culture of associations. There will be shifts in member perception of and loyalty to the association, differing preferences for programs and services, and different degrees of volunteer involvement.

Workforce—Securing a qualified workforce with the proper mix of business, technical, and social skills, combined with diverse life experiences, will demand greater skill, time, and effort from the association executive.

Outsourcing and Co-sourcing—Gaining maximum advantage from outsourcing or co-sourcing will require associations to carefully distinguish core from noncore functions and to identify the strategic benefits as well as the cost savings.

Competition and Alliances—An increasing vulnerability to competition will require associations to become more vigilant about new types of competitors and to seek out nontraditional allies.

Consolidation and Mergers—Because these are occurring with greater speed and unpredictability, associations will have to become more proactive to deal with the resulting chain reaction that affects revenues, services, and membership categories.

Globalization—As their members become less and less bounded by geography, time zones, culture, and language in their business and professional relationships, associations will have to redefine their boundaries accordingly.

Image Building—Increasing public scrutiny and competition will lead associations (professional and philanthropic organizations as well as trade organizations) to defend their members' credibility and promote the unique value of their services or activities.

Association characteristics, not size or type, determine future leadership.

When planning the scan panels, a second guiding hypothesis postulated that there would be differences in the trends identified (and their consequences) depending on the size and type of the organization. For example, we expected a different set of trends for small individual membership societies versus large trade associations. However, we learned that the same broad set of trends seemed to be affecting *all* associations regardless of size (small, medium, and large) and type (trade and individual membership organization) as well as location (Los Angeles, Chicago, or Washington, D.C.).

Ultimately, the effect of these trends upon an association in the future—and the most appropriate way to lead the organization into the future—can be best interpreted when studied in relation to these five association characteristics (which are explored in depth in Chapter 6):

- Organizational culture
- Organization's resources
- Life stage of the association
- The members' career development and life stage
- The business, profession, or cause being served

To understand the importance of characteristics such as resources and culture, consider two associations that are both taking a leadership role in the area of technology. The first is a 700-member state medical association located in the Midwest. The second is a national, insurance-related association that is located in the Washington, D.C., area and has more than 10,000 members. Despite their outward differences, both have been on the forefront of anticipating the Internet's emergence and using it to dramatically reduce postage and printing costs associated with member communications.

The two associations' responses were remarkably similar because of shared characteristics in terms of *resources* (both had the foresight to view the Internet as a tool for leveraging their printing and postage budget) as well as *cultures* that were receptive to change and were technology friendly. In other words, an association's ability to demonstrate technology leadership is more dependent on its culture and resources than on its size or budget.

Boards and staff need to see beyond the boundaries of their own associations.

Through their participation in the scan panels, the executives learned that their individual associations are not alone in facing massive change. For this reason, it is critical that everyone involved in leading the association—the executive, the board members, and the staff—has the ability to see the big picture. The issues and opportunities facing your organization will become clearer only when understood in the broader context. Associations will find it increasingly difficult to solve their problems in isolation—boards and staff must look beyond the boundaries of their own organizations. Dialogues and forums among associations will become essential to help us discover and explore new solutions.

We must be willing to question our most basic assumptions about associations.

In the face of massive change, there will arise numerous opportunities and ways for associations to prosper. To recognize these opportunities requires a fresh perspective that comes from the willingness to question *all* aspects of how an association does business. During the course of their time together, all of the panelists found themselves asking and exploring a series of thought-provoking questions, some of which are listed below:

- Do we even need associations in their traditional form?

- Which segment of our membership would most welcome a "revolution"?

- Is the current volunteer governance structure capable of keeping up with the increasingly complex decision-making environment of our association?

- Should an association CEO challenge every one of his or her members to get online within the next year?

- How much of the skill areas currently covered by ASAE's Certified Association Executive certification will be relevant five years from now?

- Will your association retain its nonprofit status or voluntarily choose to become a for-profit entity?

- Can associations retain their traditional mindsets about management and governance and still meet rising member expectations?

- Will the "digital member" replace the checkbook member?

- Is the "generic association"—where one size fits all—dead?

- Will most of our staff do a significant amount of their work at home via telecommuting?

- Will it still be possible to meet the increasingly specialized needs of members by creating special interest groups within the existing association? Or will new specialty associations break away?

- What is the future of our trade show?

Pioneers are needed.

The panelists observed that innovative approaches are desperately needed in areas such as governance, finance, and organizational design. At the same time, there are virtually no role models to follow. For the most part, associations have not yet begun inventing the solutions they need for the 21st century. Consequently, a "learning by doing" mindset will be more valuable than "learning by example." Instead of asking, "How have other associations solved this problem?" boards and staff will have to ask, "What innovative solution will we invent for ourselves? How can we be a pioneer?" Organizations that wait for others to go first will be left far behind.

Leadership is essential.

Most important, the panelists spoke passionately about the need for leadership from both the staff executive and the board. As one panelist stated, "All this talk about trends is useless unless we have the leadership to make things happen. Facing the future is more than an intellectual exercise!"

Sorting Out the Implications

Aᴅᴍɪᴛᴛᴇᴅʟʏ, the information in this report can be overwhelming. However, the future implications for your association will begin to make sense if you look at three key areas:

1. Implications of Technology

The single greatest opportunity that presents itself to association executives is the networking of knowledge—the creation and leveraging of knowledge amongst your members.
– Tᴏᴍ Pᴇᴛᴇʀꜱ, ꜱᴘᴇᴀᴋɪɴɢ ᴀᴛ ᴛʜᴇ 1993 ASAE Aɴɴᴜᴀʟ Mᴇᴇᴛɪɴɢ

Thanks to technology, interactivity at every level of the association will be enhanced. To better understand the unique implications of technology for associations, we interviewed several leading experts to paint a clearer picture of what is to come.

At the risk of resorting to hyperbole, technology will revolutionize how people and organizations interact with one another. At the 1997 ASAE Foundation New Horizons Think Tank, Nigel Burton of Microsoft noted, "The combination of the PC and the Internet is the most revolutionary thing to happen to business in the last 100 years. However important you believe these developments to be, you will probably underestimate the impact they will have." It is Burton's belief that the Internet is a driving force in the "evolution of the Information Age" and this will be, for all intents and purposes, "the next Industrial Revolution."

We are rapidly becoming a globally interconnected, highly collaborative, knowledge sharing society. The future for associations lies with new forms of interactivity.

Four technological developments with the power to transform associations:

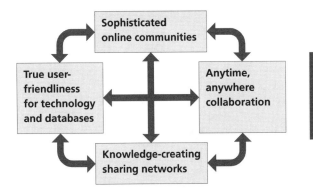

We are already seeing many practical applications in each of these development areas and can expect full practicality within 5 to 10 years.

As a result...
Interactivity at every level of the association will be revolutionized:

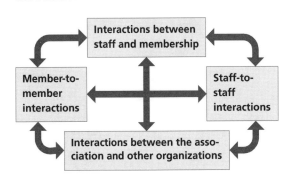

Associations live and breathe communications and interactivity in these relationship areas. They represent four points where the leveraging of knowledge and interactivity will be revolutionized by technology.

2. Major Realignments

There are many ways to analyze and work with the information from the environmental scan. One option is to analyze the effects upon your association by asking the questions in the five inter-related areas illustrated on the diagram below. The boxes represent major areas where significant shifts are prone to occur, such as a realignment in whom the association represents or serves. These areas are explored in further detail on the next two pages. At the center lies the ultimate question for associations: What will be the future relevancy of their mission?

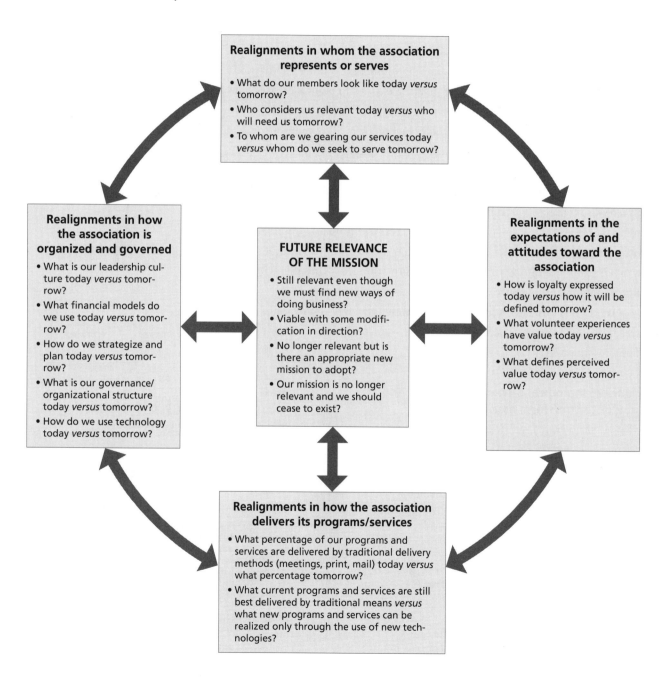

Realignments in whom the association represents or serves

- What do our members look like today *versus* tomorrow?
- Who considers us relevant today *versus* who will need us tomorrow?
- To whom are we gearing our services today *versus* whom do we seek to serve tomorrow?

Realignments in how the association is organized and governed

- What is our leadership culture today *versus* tomorrow?
- What financial models do we use today *versus* tomorrow?
- How do we strategize and plan today *versus* tomorrow?
- What is our governance/organizational structure today *versus* tomorrow?
- How do we use technology today *versus* tomorrow?

FUTURE RELEVANCE OF THE MISSION

- Still relevant even though we must find new ways of doing business?
- Viable with some modification in direction?
- No longer relevant but is there an appropriate new mission to adopt?
- Our mission is no longer relevant and we should cease to exist?

Realignments in the expectations of and attitudes toward the association

- How is loyalty expressed today *versus* how it will be defined tomorrow?
- What volunteer experiences have value today *versus* tomorrow?
- What defines perceived value today *versus* tomorrow?

Realignments in how the association delivers its programs/services

- What percentage of our programs and services are delivered by traditional delivery methods (meetings, print, mail) today *versus* what percentage tomorrow?
- What current programs and services are still best delivered by traditional means *versus* what new programs and services can be realized only through the use of new technologies?

Realignments in whom the association represents or serves

▼ FROM	▼ TO
Mature/World War II generation	Boomers and Xers
Little diversity	Multicultural diversity
Few members "E-capable"	Majority of members "E-capable" (or "E-capable" segments)
Attention on dues-paying members	Focus includes members, customers, and stakeholders
Members traditionally served (i.e., "core members")	New categories and definitions of members
Serving broad-based membership (or narrow segments)	Serving narrow segments (or broad-based membership)
Serving primarily members	Serving primarily customers
U.S.-focused association with some international members	A truly international organization with a global mindset and culture

Realignments in the expectations of and attitudes toward the association

▼ FROM	▼ TO
Loyalty to the association	Loyalty to individual/career needs
Volunteering is a privilege and duty, I give my time freely to the association	My time is valuable—make sure you use my talents wisely
Association seen as sole provider	Choices available from other sources and competitors
Members get products and programs	Members value experiences
Gathering lots of information	Seeking key insights and wisdom
New programs and services offered on an occasional basis	New programs offered continuously and "on-demand"
Buy publications and services off the shelf	Tailored to my specific needs (i.e., one-to-one marketing and mass customization)
Represent my interests through voting privileges, committees, and the board structure	Meet my needs by researching my special interests
Keep me current with today's events	Get me ready for five years out

Note: These shifts do not represent universal trends applicable to all associations nor are they intended as predictions. Instead, they are intended to direct your attention to the *potential* shifts that may shape your association's future.

Realignments in how the association delivers its programs/services

▼ FROM	▼ TO
Reliance on meetings, print publications, and mail	Wide range of options for publishing, communication, and interactivity
Static information and one-way communication	Dynamic information and interactivity
Education delivered primarily at meetings	Education anytime, anywhere via online, CD-ROM, etc.
Provider-driven education	Learner-driven education
Communication via mail	Communication via e-mail, listservs, and interactive Web sites
Member-to-member interaction limited to face-to-face venues	Interaction as an "anytime, anyplace experience" via Internet and videoconferencing
Networking organized around traditional membership categories	Networking driven by self-organizing, fluid, ad hoc groups
Meeting product "spin-offs" limited to print and audiocassettes	Meeting "experience" available to "nonattendees" and captured for later use
Traditional lobbying	Instant, more inclusive grassroots
Traditional, "time-challenged" publishing and high-cost distribution	Instant publishing and low-cost distribution via digital, electronic, online publishing
Segmented products and services	Mass customization

Realignments in how the association is organized and governed

▼ FROM	▼ TO
Management	Leadership
Governance	Visioning
Managing financial reserves	Making strategic investments for the association's future
Risk containment	Taking risks and learning from failures
Standing committees	Ad hoc task forces
Fighting the competition	Building supercharged alliances
Traditional headquarters	Virtual associations
Headquarters in control	Collaboration/partnership with grassroots chapters
Traditional staffing patterns	Patterns based on core staff, outsource partners, and temporary workers
Planning for a single preferred future	Planning for multiple futures
Command-and-control hierarchy	Team-based, networked organizations
Volunteer work done in face-to-face settings	Anytime, anywhere collaboration
Nonprofit mindset	For-profit mindset
501(c)(3) or 501(c)(6) tax-exempt status	New financial structures to best meet member needs

3. The New Rules of Planning

Create is the operative word. Create means you have to design and
work through things you've never thought of or done before…
If you see the future, you get the future;
if you see the past, you get the past.

– ED BARLOW, FUTURIST,
SPEAKING AT THE 1997 ASAE FOUNDATION NEW HORIZONS THINK TANK

In their efforts to capitalize on the profound changes before them, associations must guard against using old ways of thinking and strategizing to interpret the trends and envision their implications. They must pay particular attention to the process by which strategic planning is carried out. Mastering the new "rules" for strategic planning is a requirement for creating the future.

Rule 1: Use scenarios to envision multiple futures (the future is not an extrapolation of the past)

In *Learning from the Future: Competitive Foresight Scenarios,* Brian Marsh observes, "Good scenarios always challenge and surprise. Bad scenarios…merely confirm the prejudices of the management…."

In an age of transformation, associations must learn to imagine futures that are very different from the present reality to which they are accustomed. The old models of planning were based on the assumption that the future was predictable as an extrapolation of the present and the past:

Extrapolation and prediction

In contrast, scenario planning deliberately challenges linear thinking: It requires you to imagine two or three future scenarios. Each scenario must:

- Present an alternative image of the future instead of extrapolating present data and circumstances.
- Challenge the old assumptions of boards and staff by asking them to think the unthinkable.
- Be distinctly different from the other future scenarios.
- Be plausible because it incorporates trends known to be shaping the future.

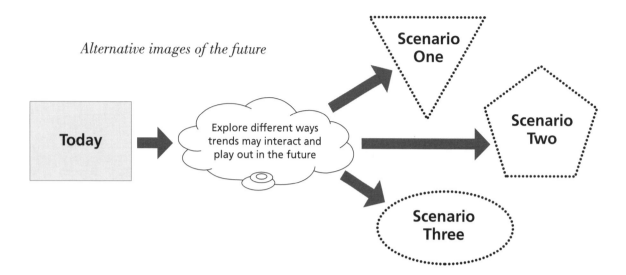

Alternative images of the future

Rule 2: Work from the future backward

Adopting new modes of strategic thinking is required before an association can create its future. Traditional strategic planning models, while appropriate for building upon past assumptions and plans, are simply inadequate for the challenges that await.

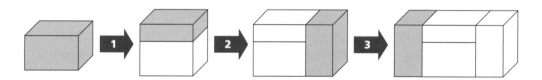

Traditional planning is appropriate for making incremental improvements

In contrast, new methods of planning require associations to first envision the future, then "rip back" to the present and determine a course of action that will lead the association in a new direction.

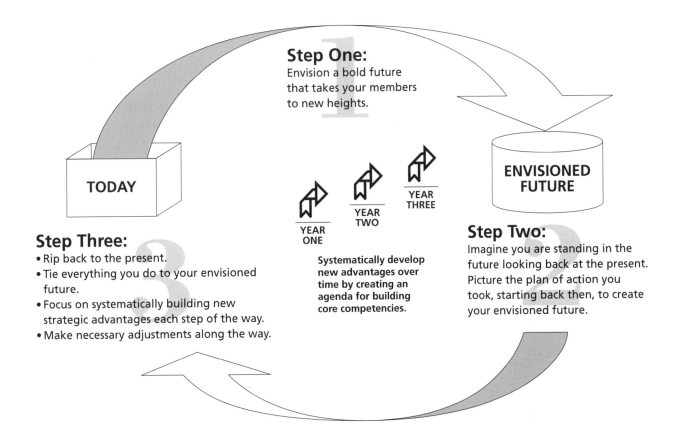

Step One:
Envision a bold future that takes your members to new heights.

ENVISIONED FUTURE

YEAR ONE

YEAR TWO

YEAR THREE

Systematically develop new advantages over time by creating an agenda for building core competencies.

TODAY

Step Two:
Imagine you are standing in the future looking back at the present. Picture the plan of action you took, starting back then, to create your envisioned future.

Step Three:
• Rip back to the present.
• Tie everything you do to your envisioned future.
• Focus on systematically building new strategic advantages each step of the way.
• Make necessary adjustments along the way.

Rule 3: Beware the misleading edge of change

It might be tempting to examine the changes discussed in Chapter 1 and interpret them as previews of how associations will look and operate in 5 to 10 years. If we lived in a world where linear extrapolation could be applied, this might be true. Many aspects of the future, however, are not apparent. For example, any assumptions based on the initial use of e-mail to communicate with members does not give a true picture of an association's future, where online collaboration is ubiquitous. The former approach simply extends the metaphor of traditional mail; while the latter helps us imagine entirely new forms of doing work, organizing volunteers, and interacting with members.

Thus, we must shift our thinking about the changes we are currently seeing in two ways:

Shifts in our thinking:

FROM ▼   **TO ▼**

The changes we are seeing provide an accurate picture of the future.	These changes contain *cues* about how the future might unfold.
The changes we are seeing represent "best practices" to be emulated.	These changes represent experiments and learning experiences.

Building on What You Have

To achieve greatness, start where you are,
use what you have, do what you can.
— Arthur Ashe

This report emphasizes the need for transformation and redesign. That focus, however, does not imply that an association should completely throw away its current structures or traditions and start all over again. That is neither feasible nor advisable. Associations have many inherent strengths and noble traditions that need to be maintained into the next century. The real challenge, therefore, is to hold onto the right strengths and traditions while finding new ways of doing business.

In *Charting Assured Migration Paths to the Knowledge Age*, Donald Norris offers the following advice: "Attempting to change the entire organizational culture generally creates a transformation initiative that is a mile wide and three inches deep. Focused change has proven to be a better tactic.... When these changes are successful, leadership must transfer that new DNA to other parts of the organization."

The chart on the next page illustrates the old and the new rules that apply to strategic thinking.

▼ Old Rules	▼ New Rules
Emphasis is on producing a strategic planning document.	**The art of strategic dialogue and collaboration is practiced.**
Planning is done at regular intervals—usually on a five-year cycle.	**Planning is an ongoing learning process that never ends.**
Scanning the environment for trends is sporadic.	**Environmental scanning is given the highest priority; adjustments are made as needed, on an ongoing basis.**
Future is explained as a logical evolution of the present; a single "most likely" future is forecasted.	**Incremental change is challenged while multiple futures are explored.**
Traditional SWOT criteria (Strengths, Weaknesses, Opportunities, and Threats) are sufficient to guide the strategy-making process.	**A creative search for emerging opportunities and deliberate abandonment of old assumptions about strengths and weaknesses is practiced.**
Board and staff engage infrequently in strategic dialogues about the future.	**Board and staff are highly collaborative and continuously engage in a dialogue about an uncertain future.**

Getting Ready for the Future

34

FACING THE FUTURE

DESPITE THE UNCERTAINTIES AND RISKS the future holds, associations will be in a position to thrive in the coming years. Take a few moments to reflect on the following four areas as they relate to your association, the strengths its possesses, and its potential greatness:

► **Leadership.** The next 5 to 10 years will be a period of intense changes and challenges for our society. Consequently, people will need leadership from their associations more than ever. Helping your members navigate through these uncertain times with potent information will generate immense value for them—and loyalty to the association. Associations will have unprecedented opportunities to influence and lead by sharing knowledge developed especially for their members.

► **Technology.** Technology is a unique and powerful tool for associations because it will revolutionize traditional functions such as communication, education, and advocacy. The interactivity fostered by the technology is the key: Members will benefit due to greater responsiveness and personalized service. As one Microsoft executive has said, "Associations live and breathe communications! And there is no area where technology has as many visible implications and benefits as in communications."

► **Membership.** With the far-reaching changes occurring in the business landscape, it is important to remember associations have a critical resource that for-profit corporations lack—*members.* The sense of community and allegiance found between an association and its members are unique qualities often missing in the for-profit sector. In associations, people willingly come together to accomplish, preserve, or advance a cause, a profession, or an industry. Together, they accomplish something that one person alone cannot.

► **Interaction.** As the proliferation of communication technology increases, the desire for human interaction will intensify. It is in this area, face-to-face interaction, where associations have traditionally focused and where their core competencies lie. The future holds the opportunity for an explosion of personalized, self-selected interactions among members facilitated by their associations. The human factor will be more important than ever.

The coming years are full of promise. The changes occurring are positive and exciting. Those associations that champion change and embrace leadership, technology, membership, and interaction will have a secure place in the future.

During times of realignment, perspective is worth fifty IQ points!
– Gary Hamel, "Strategy as Revolution,"
Harvard Business Review, July/August 1996

The next 5 to 10 years will be a period of unprecedented change for associations. To help you gain a fresher, more prescient perspective on the future, here are three "perspective shifts" to help guide your association through a time of realignment.

Perspective Shift: Look for the warning signs of incrementalism.

History shows that technologies, industries, organizations, and management concepts all have finite life spans. Toward the end of those life spans, it becomes increasingly difficult to make progress using traditional approaches. As Richard Foster notes in *The Attacker's Advantage*, "If you are at the limit, no matter how hard you try you cannot make progress. As you approach the limits, the cost of making progress accelerates dramatically."

When the limits of incremental progress have been reached, warning signs begin to emerge. They include the following:

- New competitors or providers are emerging. Some have unique strengths or competencies that your association finds difficult to match.
- Staff work harder and try to do more with existing resources.
- Traditional, tried-and-true approaches to solve problems no longer seem to work.
- It is never just one problem, but several problems at once.
- The need escalates for innovative, even unorthodox, solutions and approaches.
- There's a willingness, even an eagerness, to question the basic assumptions about how associations are governed and organized.

Is *your* association reaching the limits of incremental progress?

Perspective Shift: Assess your board's and staff's readiness to tackle the future.

Challenge your board and staff by having them complete the following "Future Self-Assessment." The results may help them determine whether they are ready to tackle the coming changes and blaze a path to the future.

Future Self-Assessment

1. Are the board and staff better at *tinkering* with old programs and services or *creating* fundamentally new ones?

0   1   2   3   4   5

Tinkering   Creating

2. To what extent do the board and staff feel they are working on a *laundry list* of tasks versus having a *compelling agenda* for creating the future?

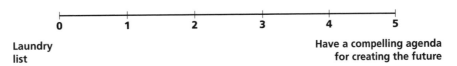

0   1   2   3   4   5

Laundry   Have a compelling agenda
list   for creating the future

3. To what extent are we guardians of the status quo or change agents?

0   1   2   3   4   5

Guardians of   Change
status quo   agents

4. To what extent do we have a vivid description of what benefits will make a meaningful difference in the lives of our members in *five years* versus today?

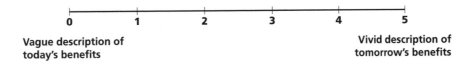

0   1   2   3   4   5

Vague description of   Vivid description of
today's benefits   tomorrow's benefits

5. To what extent are the criteria used to measure board and staff performance *externally focused* and *future-oriented* versus *internally focused* and *today-oriented*?

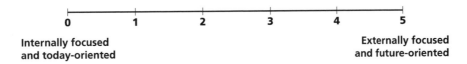

0   1   2   3   4   5

Internally focused   Externally focused
and today-oriented   and future-oriented

6. To what extent are the board and staff excited by the future and responding by raising their performance to a higher level?

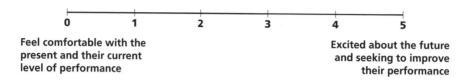

Feel comfortable with the present and their current level of performance

Excited about the future and seeking to improve their performance

7. To what extent do the board and staff monitor and discuss the trends shaping the future of the industry or profession?

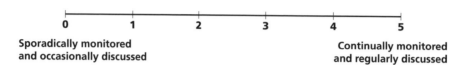

Sporadically monitored and occasionally discussed

Continually monitored and regularly discussed

8. To what extent do the board and staff monitor and discuss the trends affecting all associations and the implications for their own association?

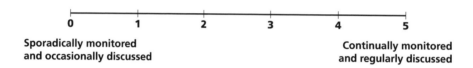

Sporadically monitored and occasionally discussed

Continually monitored and regularly discussed

9. To what extent do the board and staff use scenario building to envision multiple futures rather than forecasting a single, most likely future?

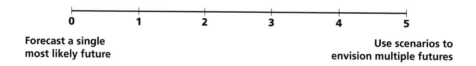

Forecast a single most likely future

Use scenarios to envision multiple futures

10. To what extent do the board and staff collaborate (i.e., actually work together) to deal with issues 1-9 listed above versus simply communicate about them?

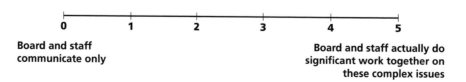

Board and staff communicate only

Board and staff actually do significant work together on these complex issues

Perspective Shift: Search for the "Berlin Walls" in your association's future.

How close is your association to experiencing a massive, even revolutionary, change? Are you even considering the possibility of this occurring within the next few years?

At the 1997 ASAE Foundation Think Tank, Peter Uberroth warned association executives about the need to stay alert for imminent change. He provided a powerful example of how quickly events can unfold, leaving leaders struggling to catch up.

Uberroth spoke of a trip to West Germany in 1989 where he was part of a group that met with Chancellor Helmut Kohl. During that meeting someone asked, "Will the Berlin Wall ever come down?" The Chancellor replied, "Yes, but not in my lifetime." *Three weeks later* the wall came down! Uberroth observed how the leaders of West Germany were that close to the situation but entirely missed both the magnitude of what was to come and the opportunity to lead.

What are the "Berlin Walls" in your association's future?

The Findings

CHAPTER

14 Trends Shaping Associations

The ASSOCIATION EXECUTIVES who participated in the Environmental Scan Panels identified 14 trends shaping associations. These trends serve as a starting point for your association and provide a "road map" to think about the future. Additionally, this road map comes with the following set of "road signs" posted by your colleagues who served as panelists.

- All the trends are directly related to one another—they must be worked simultaneously.

- The trends are best mastered in an ongoing conversation. Explore them during dialogues with leaders.

- All associations will be affected—the organization's specific size and type are not the criteria.

- Continuous investigation and probing are required. Role models and pioneers are badly needed.

- Associations are primed for change. Plan for your future now—no waiting in line is necessary.

And the most critical road sign of all:

- A leadership mindset is essential. Anything less is merely tinkering with the future.

Note: In Appendix B you'll find instructions for conducting a "future scan dialogue session," which will assist your board and staff in beginning to explore the future.

For each of the 14 trends identified by the panelists, you will find three elements:

- **The Findings.** This section provides an overview of the essential points of which board and staff should be aware.

- **Discussion and Exploration.** In this section you'll find one or two suggested topics for in-depth inquiry. These are offered as a starting point for dialogue among boards and staff. There are, of course, no right or wrong answers.

- **Potential Shifts.** This section illustrates shifts or realignments that may occur in your association as these trends take hold. These are intended to be provocative, not definitive. It is our hope they will open your thinking to dramatic changes that may occur in the next few years.

Leadership's Role

▶ *Adopting a new set of leadership characteristics will be the first step for association boards and staff as they move into the 21st century.*

The Findings

The panelists defined the leadership characteristics required of board, staff, and chief executives to manage change successfully in their associations. These characteristics are:

- **The ability to pioneer new ways of doing business.** The ASAE Foundation's research makes it clear that while many associations are struggling to change, virtually none has fully made the transition to the Knowledge Age. No role models currently exist within the association community—instead of waiting for other associations to develop new ways of doing business, a board and staff must be willing to create their own solutions.

- **The willingness to live with risks and deal with uncertainty.** The role of leadership in associations will no longer be to avoid risks but to acknowledge and find ways to exploit uncertainty. Maintaining the status quo in a time of rapid change can be the riskiest strategy of all. Exploration, experimentation, and the willingness to learn from both failures and successes must become the operational mindset.

- **The capability to anticipate where the industry or profession is going before the general membership has that awareness.** While an association must reflect and represent the views of its members, it cannot serve effectively if it simply acts as a barometer of members' current needs. An association that can do no more than respond to what its members are currently demanding will quickly become a laggard. The ability to anticipate needs before they are seen or articulated by the average member is a competency that boards and staff must diligently cultivate.

- **The commitment to engage an increasingly diverse membership and workforce in a shared vision.** Collaboration is becoming essential for associations seeking to thrive in the next century. An organization's ability to deal with complex issues, mountains of information, and a confusing array of options is improved when it harnesses the intellectual and emotional energy of its board and staff and taps into the collective wisdom of a diverse membership. Better quality information and keener insights into the future arise when collaboration is an integral part of the process.

Echoing these findings, a report issued by ASAE's Task Force on Innovation, Change and Leadership makes the following observations:

- The only viable response to the change going on around our associations is to take command of our organizational change.

- The board and chief executive must work closely together to ensure successful association-change leadership. The different needs of two key constituencies—the association's membership and its staff—must be taken into consideration.

- The chief staff executive must take the lead in developing an association planning process that will actually generate strategic change initiatives.

- The chief staff executive must take the lead in creating an association culture that is "change friendly."

Discussion and Exploration

1. Consider the strengths needed and weaknesses present among your board and staff for each of the following key leadership characteristics:

LEADERSHIP CHARACTERISTICS	BOARD		STAFF	
	Strengths Needed	Weaknesses Present	Strengths Needed	Weaknesses Present
Fostering a change friendly culture.				
Ability to anticipate future member needs.				
Collaboration: the ability to engage diverse groups in shared acts of discovery and creation.				
Willingness to take risks and ability to deal with uncertainty.				
Willingness to invent new solutions when role models do not yet exist in other associations.				

2. Consider how the leadership function will be shared between the board and chief executive in your association.

The Drucker Foundation has identified three roles for today's leaders: pathfinding, aligning, and empowering. Given that association leadership is a responsibility shared by the board and chief executive, how should collaboration evolve over the next three to five years? What strengths can you build on? What obstacles do you need to overcome?

Three roles of the leader	How will the board and chief executive share and/or separate these roles in the future?
Pathfinding: A compelling vision and mission tied to the needs of (members) customers and stakeholders.	
Aligning: Structure systems, processes, and people to contribute to achieving the mission and vision.	
Empowering: The purpose and mission of each person is commingled with that of the organization and the talent, ingenuity, intelligence, and creativity of staff is unleashed.	

Potential Shifts

▼ FROM	▼ TO
Management	Leadership
Maintaining traditions	Confronting the real barriers to transformation, innovation, and invention
Risk containment	Taking risks and learning from failures
Focusing on day-to-day details	Building a shared vision
Researching existing best practices	Innovation and pioneering new ways of doing business
Micromanagement	Empowerment
Acting as a membership barometer	Guiding members on the path to the future

Value/Return on Investment (ROI)

▶ *Meeting rising member expectations and a greater demand for a return on the dues investment will drive association redesign.*

The Findings

The panelists confirmed that associations are dealing with rising member expectations. If an association isn't demonstrating its value on an ongoing basis, another organization—either nonprofit or for-profit—will step in and provide more value. This trend poses a four-fold challenge for associations.

- **Understanding the new standards of performance for the Knowledge Age.** Associations need to understand the key drivers of value. For example, members will demand mass customization and one-to-one marketing of information-related products. In the realm of education, the demand for "just in time" and "on demand" programs will dominate. Associations that deliver educational experiences in which members can partake while at the office or when traveling (i.e., fuse work with learning) will win the value game. As a result, the ability to deliver quality education in "snippets" will be as important as delivering all-day programs.

- **Developing a clearly defined value proposition.** Associations must carefully choose whom they will serve (i.e., a broad-based membership versus one or more narrow segments) and the range of programs and services to offer (e.g., a broad range versus a specialized array of programs and services). At the same time, they must guard against trying to be "all things to all members." As a result, many will find it necessary to move their value proposition from one quadrant to another, as illustrated below:

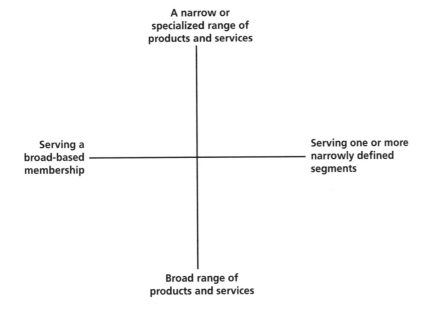

A narrow or specialized range of products and services

Serving a broad-based membership

Serving one or more narrowly defined segments

Broad range of products and services

- **Continuously focusing on improving quality.** Programs and services must not only be carefully targeted, but also perceived by members as being of high quality and superior value compared to offerings from competitors. Today's standards for quality will not suffice in five years. Continuous quality improvement will increasingly drive member satisfaction.

- **Creating value by nurturing intellectual capital.** As associations enter the Knowledge Age they must devote careful attention to how they manage their intellectual capital. Of interest is the emerging field of "knowledge management" that allows organizations to share and recycle corporate knowledge (e.g., best practices) and create a corporate memory.

Knowledge management has been described as "nurturing and leveraging the intellectual capital of an organization. This capital is embedded in people's heads, in processes, and in relationships—the goal of an association CEO is to grow that capital for the membership, so it has value for them." Knowledge deployment is not only necessary but also already possible, because knowledge workers can be interconnected through networks.

Executives will have to study carefully how their members interact and use the information provided by the association to create new knowledge. They will have to think about how to manage those interactions and the process of knowledge creation to create the greatest possible leverage. There are four main points of interaction to address: interaction among members, among staff, between staff and members, and between the association and other organizations.

Discussion and Exploration

1. How will you measure your members' perceived value?

- What methods will you use? Will it be an objective measurement (based on quantitative and qualitative research) or the subjective opinion of board and staff?

- Do you measure perceived value among the various segments within your membership (for example, are you asking all segments within your membership for their point of view)? Do you know which segments are the most satisfied with their membership? The least satisfied? Why?

- Which products and services have the highest satisfaction or quality ratings? The lowest?

- Do you know what specific factors influence your members' perception of value?

- Which quadrant best describes your current value proposition?

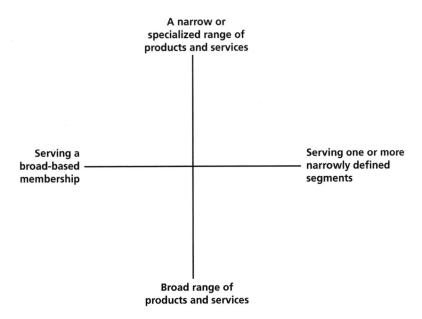

2. Are you identifying the factors that will change your members' perception of value over the next three to five years?

Can you anticipate which factors are altering members' expectations? For example, in the next three to five years, will your members expect:

- One-to-one customization of information services and publications?
- More and faster services via the Internet?
- Meetings and services highly targeted to special interest areas?
- A virtual trade show?
- Video conference training programs or online education?

What other areas are you investigating? Who are you asking: Current members? Potential members? Former members?

Potential Shifts

▼ FROM	▼ TO
Measuring retention rates and net growth	Measuring member satisfaction and relevance of the association
Product and programs decisions based on subjective opinions of volunteers and staff	Objective decision making, guided by market research
Mass marketing	Mass customization/one-to-one marketing
Static information (e.g., publications, reports)	Dynamic information—interactivity that creates new knowledge
Members receive products and programs	Members value knowledge, insights, and experiences
Access to broad, unfiltered information	Knowledge navigation and synthesis

Responsiveness

▶ *Keeping up with external changes and responding rapidly to members' emerging needs will require associations to become fast, fluid, and flexible.*

The Findings

The panelists uncovered two ways that responsiveness will be critical to associations in the future. The first is *internal* responsiveness: focusing on members' needs and their time frames. The second is *external* responsiveness: being fluid and flexible in response to changes in the outside environment. There is no point in scanning the environment if your association cannot respond quickly to emerging opportunities, partnerships, or competition.

To be responsive, associations need to do the following:

- **Increase the capacity to monitor members' needs as they emerge.** Annual mailed-out surveys will not suffice when it is feasible to use the Internet for rapid, targeted, and ongoing monitoring of nascent issues and needs among your members. For example, Microsoft has been working with the National PTA to help connect its national and state offices. This has made a substantial difference in the organization's ability to communicate key issues to their members and gather feedback.

- **Introduce new products and services faster.** Panelists observed that their associations must compress product-development cycles. One participant noted that his association was rolling out a new member service every six weeks!

- **Retire old programs faster.** Along with faster roll-outs, associations must also have an effective infrastructure and evaluation process to terminate old programs quickly and efficiently.

- **"Walk the talk" on customer service.** This is especially important in a global economy where members want 24-hour access via the Web and fax-on-demand, call centers available regardless of their time zones, and overnight delivery of publications and information. Associations, like many for-profits, are never closed. This finding raises two questions:

  - To what extent does a headquarters-centric mentality dictate service availability? For example, does your association subject its members to "time zone tyranny" because its service hours are more convenient for staff?

  - How well do you keep up with new developments in customer service technology? Advances in software programming are creating a new generation of tools to improve customer service. For example, the use of "case-based reasoning" can speed and enhance customer service support by identifying recurring patterns among customer requests, then automating the process for responding to the most frequently asked questions. This artificial intelligence tool is being used to create a new generation of "self-help" Web sites.

- **Make environmental scanning an ongoing activity.** Scanning the environment once every three to five years is no longer sufficient. At the ASAE Foundation Think Tank, futurist Ed Barlow offered this advice to association executives: "To keep your understanding of your industry or profession current, you will have to dedicate 20% of your time to environmental scanning."

- **Make responsiveness fundamental to partnerships.** There is an increasing need for timely decisions and quicker turnaround times. Associations' viability and desirability as partners will depend as much on their responsiveness as on the access they offer to their members. Partners are likely to shift their attitudes from "slowness is just part of doing business with associations" to "we need you to be responsive, or we will find another partner."

Discussion and Exploration

1. How are you scanning, benchmarking, and measuring?

Every association needs to collect the right information before it can gauge whether it is being responsive. To gauge internal responsiveness, are you:

- Measuring members' expectations based on their preferences and their time frames?

- Measuring the time between a customer complaint and your response to it?

- Benchmarking your responsiveness in the area of customer service in comparison with competitors and partners?

- Keeping up with state-of-the-art developments in customer service?

To gauge external responsiveness, you need to know the rate of change in the environment outside your association. Are you using environmental scanning to measure the external rate of change?

2. How are you analyzing the factors that determine responsiveness in your association?

- *Information flow.* Is information quickly shared throughout the entire organization to facilitate a speedy response? Where does the flow slow down?

- *Processes and procedures.* Are they designed for internal convenience or service delivery? Who is the real customer?

- *Decision-making autonomy.* Who has authority to act quickly and decisively in dealing with members, customers, and partners?

- *People.* Consider the culture of your board and staff; is your organization truly oriented toward member/customer service?

Potential Shifts

▼ FROM	▼ TO
Maintaining old programs indefinitely	Retiring programs as soon as they are irrelevant
Extensive research and lead times for program/product development (months or years)	Expedited marketing and compressed development cycles (weeks or months)
Bureaucratic decision-making processes involving volunteers	Fast, fluid, flexible processes and decision-making autonomy for staff
Favoring a headquarters-centric mentality	Service criteria determined by end users' needs
Staff culture directed toward serving the board	Staff culture primarily focused on serving grassroots members
Toll-free member service hotlines	Self-help Web sites using the next generation of customer service software

Governance

▶ *The inability of current governance models to deal with an increasingly complex, fast-paced environment will require a cultural shift for most associations.*

The Findings

The panelists made three important observations about association governance:

- **Current governance models are outmoded and obsolete.** The current model for governing the structure and process of associations is too slow and cumbersome to deal with an increasingly complex, fast-paced environment. The times call for a dramatic and innovative restructuring.

  An ASAE Foundation study currently in progress, titled *Association Governance, Structure, & Culture: Best Practices*, notes that "Twenty-first century associations are laboring with 19th century structures.... Process often strangles effective, timely decisions on substantive issues and is often reinvented annually." Consensus Management Group, based in Harriman, New York, is conducting the research. It uncovered a number of "works in progress" but found that it is too soon to measure their effectiveness. In other words, the associations in the study are just beginning to create new models of governance for the next century. Other observations from the research include:

  - There is no one right way or "one size fits all" approach to structure or governance. Too many associations are looking for a plug-and-play approach to organizational design. They first must ask fundamental questions about what business they are in, the needs of their members, environmental factors, and the capacity of the association to change.

  - Associations want to change the bylaws at the first sign of difficulty (such as declining numbers of volunteers or increasing cost of governance) rather than think through the issues in determining whether function or form needs to be addressed.

  - Associations pay little attention to how their culture influences "the way we do business around here," preferring instead to make changes in structure or governance.

  - Members are rarely interested in association structure and governance. Leaders and staff are the ones most often concerned with these issues.

  - In too few instances do associations ask "What will success look like?" as a result of changes in governance or organizational design. Defensible evaluation criteria are rarely established before the process is initiated.

- **Future boards must focus on member value and organize for responsiveness.** Associations will need to create new governance forms based on collaborative and flexible processes that focus on delivering increased value to members within a shortened time frame. The use of technology will play a key role in enabling boards to communicate and collaborate in between face-to-face meetings.

- **The composition of the board must reflect the future of the membership.** Board composition is increasingly an essential element in an association's ability to look forward. The proper mix of future, current, and historical perspectives will be required. The board must be composed to balance three issues:

  - How to reflect the future diversity of the membership, 5 to 10 years out, in terms of generation, gender, ethnic composition, and experience level.

  - How to adequately represent the current membership.

  - How to retain a historical perspective and lessons learned from previous boards.

Discussion and Exploration

1. **What will "success" look like? Which of the following outcomes does your association seek as a result of changes in its governance structure and process?**

   - Create greater value for members.

   - Improve the organization's ability to scan the environment for changes and anticipate future member needs.

   - Strengthen the organization's ability to make complex decisions more wisely.

   - Represent the increased diversity of the membership.

   - Other: _____

2. **How will you explore ways to redesign your governance system?**

   Given that current governance models are obsolete and new models have yet to be created, association executives must guide their associations toward building a new governance model.

Potential Shifts

▼ FROM	▼ TO
Traditional political agendas and internal focus	Anticipating members' needs in the future and changes in the environment
Low-performance boards	High-performance boards
Internally focused accountability measures	Board held accountable for creating member value
Streamlining the board to achieve incremental gains in efficiency	Reinventing governance to excel in the 21st century
Technology restrained	Technology competency as basic leadership criteria
Changing the bylaws to fix today's problems	Altering the board culture for future flexibility
Board and volunteer leadership relatively homogeneous	Diversity rules

Revenue Sources

▶ *Associations must be willing to retire historically profitable programs and services in favor of creating new programs. They also need to extend their traditional areas of expertise (i.e., core competencies) to create new revenue-generating programs.*

The Findings

The following factors appear to be changing the revenue formula for associations:

- **Shifting from "reactive marketing" to "prescient marketing."**
  In the past, associations could rely on a simple and proven technique to determine what new products and services to introduce: Ask the members. That approach is no longer adequate for keeping up with the rapid pace of today's and tomorrow's marketplaces. As a result, associations must shift their marketing mindset to the right-hand side of the diagram below:

Members know the solution to their problem and ask the association to deliver it.	Members know they have a problem but don't know the solution. Association must imagine and deliver the solution on their behalf.	Members lack the foresight to see a future problem or opportunity. Association must imagine and prepare solution in advance of members' awareness.
Reactive Marketing	**Responsive Marketing**	**Prescient Marketing**

- **Taking new financial approaches that focus on long-term investments in core competencies.** To succeed in tomorrow's markets, associations must start investing in new sets of core competencies—the skills and capabilities that make an organization uniquely qualified to serve its members or customers. For example, an association might choose to develop a core competency in building "knowledge networks" among its members (see the Technology Usage trend).

  Achieving mastery of a core competency, especially one that will create value in the Knowledge Age, takes years not months. Thus, some associations are relinquishing the old mindset (which seeks relatively quick paybacks from profitable programs and services) in favor of new financial approaches that account for the lag time associated with investing in a core competency and reaping its financial benefits.

- **Seeking breakthrough products and services through expeditionary marketing practices.** A few associations have abandoned the traditional process of product and program development, which involves volunteer committees and long lead times before market introduction.

Instead they are finding that expeditionary marketing—rapidly creating prototype products and services that serve as low-cost probes into the future—is the best and fastest way to learn what the market wants. It's essentially a form of "guerrilla marketing," where the reconnaissance is built into the product or service.

Compared to traditional market research methods, this is a faster and more accurate way to gauge members' needs. The emphasis is on creating "sticky" prototypes that can capture information on members' needs, which in turn is used in a process of continuous improvement. As an example, one association is literally turning out a new information-based product every six weeks.

As associations shift to expeditionary marketing, they will find it increasingly necessary to decouple the governance process from the product/service development process.

• **Creating new membership categories.** Four factors lead to the creation of new membership categories:

  • *Segmentation.* New membership categories are being created to better target segments previously underserved or new segments that have recently evolved among the membership.

  • *Extension.* New categories bring in different types of members, such as public memberships, suppliers, and related professions.

  • *The Internet.* Given the ubiquity of technology, Web-only memberships are feasible.

  • *Realignment.* New membership structures respond to major shifts in an industry or profession brought on by mergers and consolidations.

• **Reassessing the traditional revenue formula (dues versus *à la carte* services).** Associations are rethinking what percentage of their programs and services could be offered *à la carte* on a for-fee basis and what parts should be included with the membership dues. Some associations will find it advantageous to increase their dependence on dues because of the value of the overall membership package they have to offer. Other associations will go in the opposite direction and may even consider the possibility of abandoning membership dues and rely on for-fee services (developing a "customer base" rather than a "membership base").

Discussion and Exploration

1. Consider these two questions in concert, and brainstorm what entirely new revenue sources you might pursue or create:

Expeditionary Products and Services	Supercharged Alliances
Expeditionary Products and Services Make a list of expeditionary products or services you could launch within the next two months. What prototypes can you quickly develop and test? For example, can you identify the most valuable information or knowledge you currently offer to your members and quickly test four new ways to deliver it, such as via a Web site, electronic newsletter, fax, and videoconferencing?	**Supercharged Alliances** With whom could you develop a supercharged alliance to gain an essential competency? For example: • A university with experience building virtual campuses and interactive learning experiences? • A company like Firefly that has developed the technology for creating sophisticated, online communities? • A customized news retrieval provider, such as Individual Inc., that has mastered the technical aspects of one-to-one marketing?

Note: This exercise is based on presentations and publications done by Donald Norris, Strategic Initiatives, Inc.

2. What future revenue formulas will you explore for your association?

Assess your current revenue formula using the grid below. Then imagine two other revenue formulas that are radically different from the current one (for instance, shifting from a majority of revenue from dues to revenue entirely from fee-based services—or to having 70% of your revenue come from new products and services). Under what scenarios would these radical new revenue formulas become plausible or advantageous?

Revenue from dues	Revenue from *à la carte*/fee offerings	
Dues from new members and/or categories _____%	Current products/services sold to new members/customers _____%	New products/services sold to new members/customers _____%
Dues from current membership base _____%	Current products/services sold to current member/customer base _____%	New products/services sold to current member/customer base _____%

Total Equals 100%

Potential Shifts

▼ FROM	▼ TO
Maintaining the financial reserves	Making strategic investments in new core competencies for long-term payoffs
Dues (bundled services)	New revenue models (*à la carte*/pay as you go)
Milking old programs past their prime	Developing new core competencies that lead to a host of new programs
Recruiting new members similar to current members	Creating new categories of members and customers
Majority of revenue from mature products/programs	Significant revenue from newly developed products/programs
Traditional sponsorships and affinity programs	Supercharged alliances and partnerships

Technology Usage

▶ *The profound and beneficial influence of technology usage will be felt through its increasing capability to link people, build relationships, and foster communities.*

The Findings

Don't lose your common sense.
Everything at the end of the wire is just other people.
— Esther Dyson, past chair, Electronic Frontier Foundation

Participants in the environmental scan panels saw the benefits of technology in very human terms. While technology is a rapidly changing and often overwhelming subject, our research uncovered five themes that you can use to explore the human element of technology's promise:

• **Monitor the technologies that will enhance your association's capabilities in the areas of community building, collaboration, and knowledge sharing.** Associations that move to the forefront of using technology with a "human touch" will reap immense benefits for members and gain tremendous competitive advantages against potential for-profit competitors. Such technologies include:

  • *Online community building technology.* At the 1997 ASAE Management & Technology Conference, Patty Maes of the Massachusetts Institute of Technology spoke about advances in intelligent software agents that are bringing a higher level of personalization to online communities. These agents can be trained to locate the tastes, opinions, preferences, and idiosyncrasies most similar to those of the individual user.

  • *Collaborative tools.* What if the members of your association could collaborate anytime, anywhere, via the Internet? What if virtual committees and task forces could be easily formed and disbanded, sharing files and voting online? What if your members and staff could interact in real time around a virtual whiteboard? These are some of the plausible, near-term developments in collaborative technologies known as "groupware" (e.g., Lotus Notes and Microsoft Exchange).

  • *Knowledge-sharing networks.* Several companies have already developed functional knowledge networks to help individuals tap into the collective intelligence of a greater community. These networks support continuous learning by accelerating the spread of best practices and best-known methods throughout the organization and by expanding the expertise available to solve specific problems, plan, or make decisions.

• **Don't underestimate the Internet.** While the Internet is arguably still under development, associations must guard against underestimating its current level of functionality or the speed at which its bandwidth capacity and overall capabilities will increase in the next three to five years. The Internet is a viable tool for all associations because the technology can be used equally well by all sizes and types of organizations.

Several associations have already reduced their telephone, postage, and publication costs by using the Internet. Other associations have successfully used the Internet to create online collaboratories, sponsor virtual trade shows, offer online education, conduct online board meetings, develop online databases for members to share technical solutions, and engage members for input before major legislative conferences.

- **Technology will become increasingly accessible and seamless to association staff.** Technology experts point to a number of advances in computer hardware and software that are making it even easier for associations to interface with computers, access data, and handle paperwork. For example, information stored in an association's database will be *malleable* or easily customizable thanks to the ongoing development of database manipulation software. This software will allow any person on staff to easily request information from a membership or financial database. Barriers to accessing and sharing information across departmental lines are being eliminated, breaking down departmental silos.

- **Expect pain, then gain, when dealing with "dual systems."** The panelists acknowledged the pain of making the transitions associated with technology. Many associations will be dealing with "dual systems" over the next few years where systems and members are somewhere between fully using new technologies and abandoning old ones (e.g., part of the membership is Internet-savvy and the rest aren't). While this creates intense short-term difficulties, associations must have the leadership to look ahead and prepare a different future.

- **The chief executive must become a "technology strategist."** For the chief executive, technology is less about the details of implementation and more about the vision and strategy. There are three facets to this:

  - *Providing leadership.* Taking full advantage of technology's promise means implementing change; an association cannot act solely as a barometer of its membership. Thus, the chief executive must be willing to get out in front and assume the risks involved.

  - *Envisioning technology as a strategic advantage, not just a tool.* Associations must be able to differentiate themselves from their competitors based on their ability to use technology.

  - *Understanding the strategic issues unique to the Internet.* This includes, for example, learning how the Internet is radically altering the cost-infrastructures of bringing members together or altering the economics of publishing and information distribution.

Discussion and Exploration

1. How are you envisioning technology as a strategic advantage for your association?

Complete the following statements:

Technology will give us a unique competitive advantage because our understanding and mastery of it will exceed that of our competitors. Here's how: _____.

We know exactly where to apply technology and how to leverage it to create the type of value most sought by our members. Here's how:

_____.

2. How do you define leadership in terms of technology?

Assess the following:

- The board's comfort and competency with technology.

- How you encourage and educate members who are fearful of technology.

- How you advance the use of technology for the widespread benefit of your industry or profession.

Potential Shifts

▼ FROM	▼ TO
E-mail as a convenient communication format	Creating high-touch, human-touch environments featuring anytime, anywhere collaboration
Disjointed, patchwork use of individual technologies	Harmonious integration and synergies
Technology as a cost	Mastery of technology to achieve strategic advantages
Member and sales data held hostage by MIS department	Database accessible to and usable by entire staff
Drowning under a mountain of paper transactions (membership forms, meeting registrations, etc.)	Time savings through E-commerce transactions

Change Loops

▶ *Mastering the unplanned changes and unexpected consequences ("change loops") that do not fall neatly inside the time frame of the traditional planning calendar or scheduled board meetings will require a new mindset about the budget and planning processes.*

The Findings

- **Unplanned changes and unexpected consequences are a fact of life.** Based on their experiences implementing change in their organizations, panelists noted a particular phenomena: For each change implemented (such as a change in membership categories), a variety of unanticipated consequences results (such as a change in dues). Each of these consequences, in turn, requires the association to implement yet another change. What results is a series of "change loops" that do not fall neatly inside the time frame of the traditional planning calendar and scheduled board meetings.

- **Associations must learn to allocate sufficient time, resources, and energy to deal with the unexpected.** In a world where unplanned changes and unexpected consequences are the norm, associations must develop a built-in capacity for making ongoing adjustments. In most of their planning and budgeting processes, the vast majority of the staff's and volunteers' time and effort is directed toward two areas: planning and implementation. But virtually no contingency is made for dealing with the "change loop" phenomena.

   Tremendous amounts of time are set aside at the beginning of each year for the budget season, and great efforts are put forth in the annual budget presentations. In contrast, far less time and effort are spent in the "back end" during the review process. Too often, insufficient time and resources are allocated for adjusting and fine tuning the plan. Yet in the future, budgeting and other processes will need to be *redesigned* to reflect the following shift:

▼ FROM	▼ TO
1. Set aside time for planning and budgeting	1. Set aside time for planning and budgeting
2. Allocate staff and volunteer time and budget for implementation	2. Allocate staff and volunteer time and budget for implementation
3. Set aside minimal time for "traditional" review process and follow-up (i.e., cross fingers and hope everything goes as planned)	3. ***Allocate sufficient staff and volunteer time and budget for making ongoing adjustments as needed** (i.e., acknowledge and be prepared in advance for unplanned consequences and unexpected events)*

To deal with change loops, associations will need to examine the following ratio:

$$\frac{\text{Percentage of time and effort allocated for planning/budgeting}}{\text{Percentage of time allocated for ongoing adjustments}}$$

Associations with a top-heavy ratio will find themselves unable to cope with the change loop phenomena.

Discussion and Exploration

1. What are the consequences of a top-heavy ratio for your organization? What needs to change?

Potential Shifts	
▼ **FROM**	▼ **TO**
Planning for certainty	Preparing for unplanned consequences and unexpected events
Build products and programs once	Build change into the product or program
Rigid, predesigned budget and planning systems	Self-adjusting and self-informing systems

Generational Issues

▶ *The generational shifts among staff, board, and members (Matures born before 1946; Boomers born between 1946 and 1964; and Generation X born between 1965 and 1985) will fundamentally alter the culture of associations. There will be shifts in member perception of and loyalty to the association, differing preferences for programs and services, and differing degrees of volunteer involvement.*

The Findings

Panelists acknowledge that this trend has already surfaced within their offices, their boards, and their membership. Three distinct generations are present: Matures (born before 1946), Boomers (born between 1946 and 1964), and Generation X (born between 1965 and 1985). Associations will need to accommodate the generational differences in terms of the content and delivery preferences for programs and services, the perception of and loyalty to the association, and the degree of volunteer involvement.

Associations should investigate three broad themes:

• **The phasing out of the mature generation means redesigning for Boomers and Xers.** In terms of numbers, the presence of Matures as members and staff is diminishing. Boomers and Xers will increasingly populate associations, and this mix will strongly influence all aspects of associations in the future. It is important to acknowledge that the governance structure, culture, and offerings of many associations are creations of and for the mature generation. What worked so well for that generation is often at odds with the lifestyle and value perceptions of Boomers and Xers.

Associations must begin redesigning themselves with the Boomer/Xer generational shift in mind. To date, little research has been done about generational differences as they relate to associations. Associations will have to investigate the following areas and consider how member preferences will change as the Matures fade out and Boomers and Xers predominate:

Areas for investigation	Potential shifts as Boomers and Xers predominate
Format and content of meetings	From longer, multi-day meetings heavy on social events to shorter, more focused meetings that require less time away from families.
Volunteering	From permanent standing committees and multi-year commitments to working on ad hoc, short-lived task forces.
Governance	From automatic respect and conformity to questioning of authority and more demand for accountability and business-like practices from boards. Less inclination by members to get involved in day-to-day management of association.
Loyalty	From a sense of joining as a "noble obligation" to membership as a career or business necessity or expense.

- **Boomers versus Xers: the next battle of the generations.** As Boomers take over management of associations, both on the staff and volunteer side, they will need to take into account their relationships with Generation X. The nature of this relationship will have a profound and long-lasting influence on associations. Panelists expressed concern that managing and engaging Xers presents a significant challenge; a situation that has been described as "the battle of the generations (the forty-somethings versus the twenty-somethings)." In general, Xers:

  - Accept change well and adapt easily.
  - Are comfortable with technology.
  - Are independent.
  - Are not intimidated by authority; many do not seek approval from those in charge.
  - Are creative and add a fresh perspective to problem solving and strategy sessions.

  Above all, Boomers may have to learn to deal with the Xers' entrepreneurial spirit: According to an IBM study, one in five small businesses today is owned by someone under the age of 35. Possible implications include: Xers within your association seeking to start and manage their own special interest groups, task forces, and meetings; or Xers banding together to start a competing specialty association or for-profit service provider.

- **Pay attention to the Net Generation.** In his book, *Growing Up Digital*, Don Tapscott discusses the next generation moving into the workforce: the Net Generation (or N-Gen). Currently between the ages of 10 and 20, they were born in the era of the Internet, just as many of us were born in an era of ubiquitous television. Association executives should make a conscious effort to learn from this generation, which is accustomed to peer collaboration, networking, and working virtually.

Discussion and Exploration

1. Examine the generational profile of your membership:

- What are the ratios of Matures to Boomers to Xers?

- Which group(s) predominate?

- Does your board and volunteer structure reflect this profile?

2. Does your association have sufficient information to determine generational differences in terms of:

- Perceived level of satisfaction?

- Types of programs and services desired and delivery preferences?

- Attitudes about meetings and time away from home or office?

- Attitudes about governance and leadership of the association?

- Loyalty to the association?

- Willingness to volunteer, motivations, and preferred time commitments?

How are you collecting this information? From what sources?

Potential Shifts

▼ FROM	▼ TO
Mature/World War II Generation	Boomers and Xers
Volunteering is a duty and privilege!	What's in it for my career development?
Time-intensive volunteer opportunities	Short-lived, highly focused volunteer opportunities
Loyalty to the association's cause and mission	Loyalty to individual/career needs
Multi-day meetings heavy on social events	Shorter, value-focused meetings
Satisfied with limited/traditional delivery methods (meetings, print, mail)	Internet-savvy members demand more options and delivery on their terms

Workforce

▶ *Securing a qualified workforce with the proper mix of business, technical, and social skills combined with diverse life experiences will demand greater skill, time, and effort.*

The Findings

The workforce of the future has been described as "mobile, digital, and very collaborative."

During the environmental scan panels, several broad themes related to the workforce emerged:

- **The effect of changing organizational design.** Associations are undergoing organizational redesign in response to the need to create organizations that are fast, flexible, and fluid. This includes a shift away from hierarchical, command-and-control structures toward more decentralized or networked organizations and increasing reliance on project-based teams. A number of associations are using the cross-functional, team-based management approach, and at least one has eliminated job titles for staff.

  In addition, technology is spurring the growth of distributed work via telecommuting and virtual offices. The distributed workforce, particularly computer-supported work, continues to expand. More than 11 million people telecommuted in 1998, compared to 8.5 million in 1995.

  These changes are forcing a "cultural realignment" for organizations. The resulting change may be difficult for some existing workers and lead to staff turnover. One chief staff executive, for example, noted that instituting organizational redesign led to a turnover of 80% of her staff. In addition, associations will have to adjust their hiring practices in order to recruit the right people to fit into the new culture.

- **An overall fragmentation of the workforce.** Workforces of the past could be characterized as "concentrated" in that most staff were full-time employees and worked onsite. Over the past 20 years the full-time workforce has fragmented. Fewer people now have permanent jobs; more are temporary, part-time, contingent, or contract workers.

  Between 1980 and 1996, the contingent workforce grew faster than the economy, and contingent workers now represent about 25% to 31% of the workforce. Temporary work grew 500% in those same years. By the year 2010, 50% of Americans may be self-employed. With telecommuting and flexible work hours factored in, associations are experiencing an overall fragmentation of the workforce that makes it harder to manage in traditional ways. (Based on information from *Managing Your Future as an Association, Thinking about Trends and Working with Their Consequences*, by Joseph Coates and Jennifer Jarratt, 1994 and 1997).

- **The need for younger workers to have both technical skills and people skills.** Associations are becoming increasingly dependent on younger employees to provide computer, MIS, Internet, and other technical skills. But will these workers have the requisite people skills that are so important to association management? Panelists acknowledged that hiring people with both sets of skills is a challenge. They are being forced to look at new and better ways to train or mentor younger workers in the people-side of association management.

- **Increased human relations (HR) sophistication in response to a more diverse workforce.** The workforce has become more diverse due to increased representation from minorities, generational segments, and gender. The panelists anticipate conflicts between the needs of tomorrow's workforce with those of today's in the following areas:

  - Career development expectations
  - Loyalty to the job and the organization
  - Lifestyle values
  - Communication and problem-solving styles

As a result, the HR function in associations will require greater skill and sophistication in its administration. All aspects of hiring, retaining, and training staff will become more complex and demanding. Associations will have to carefully evaluate their in-house capabilities and weigh the pros and cons of outsourcing the HR function.

Ultimately, associations will find that staff retention is essential to delivering increasing value to their members. As noted by ASAE's Task Force on Organizational Design, "Organizations of the future will increasingly find themselves reliant on the knowledge capabilities of their professional staff.... Knowledge is a competitive asset of the association resident with its professional staff...." Associations will have to reassess the value of their "knowledge workers" and develop new formulas for determining their employees' true worth and ability to contribute membership value.

Discussion and Exploration

1. Write the help wanted ad you will place in five years.

Which of the following criteria would you emphasize?

- The types of skills and expertise the job candidate should have.

- A definition of the right type of personality for your organization.

- A description of your organization's culture and why it is an attractive place to work?

Where should you place this ad? How is your future ad different from the ones you are placing today?

Potential Shifts

▼ FROM	▼ TO
Traditional staff patterns	"Shamrock" organization consisting of core staff, outsource partners, and temporary workers
Staff roles assigned according to hierarchy	Staff freelance inside networked, decentralized organizations
Finding someone to "just do the work"	Hiring a knowledgeable worker suited to a collaborative culture
Hiring primarily for skills geared to an existing program	Hiring the "total person," including skills, life experiences, and attitude

Outsourcing and Co-sourcing

▶ *Gaining maximum advantage from outsourcing or co-sourcing will require associations to carefully distinguish core from noncore functions and identify its strategic benefits as well as cost savings.*

The Findings

Associations will increasingly outsource many of the noncore functions traditionally performed by staff. As a result, staffs can be leaner, more flexible, and more focused on the key activities that create value for the member. Traditional assumptions about the number of core staff needed to serve a particular size membership will become increasingly less valid.

The importance of outsourcing as a way to reduce costs (i.e., services can be provided cheaper and faster out of house) will continue to support this trend. In addition, two underlying shifts are occurring to fuel the need for outsourcing and co-sourcing:

- **The intensifying need to focus on creating value means more nonessential functions will be outsourced.** In response to the Value/ROI and Responsiveness trends, associations must identify and focus on the core functions most essential to creating value. The increasing importance of managing staff as "knowledge workers" is changing how associations assess the costs and benefits of outsourcing. In the past, the emphasis was on the cost savings of outsourcing. In the future, the primary evaluation criterion for choosing to outsource/co-source will shift toward the benefits accrued by freeing staff to concentrate on activities that create knowledge and add value.

- **Expertise needed in certain specialized areas will be best obtained through outsourcing or co-sourcing.** Two factors drive this. First, in areas such as MIS, accounting, human relations, and administration, many associations will find it difficult to hire quality staff and assume the high costs for their continuing education. Outside firms are better qualified to handle these issues because their narrow focus and degree of specialization justifies investments in training and maintaining state-of-the-art practices. Second, by serving multiple clients, they can readily apply lessons learned from one association to the problems of another.

Discussion and Exploration

1. **How do you currently define and identify your association's core functions?**

    Given those core functions, what skills and competencies must reside among staff? (For instance, which are the most essential to creating value for your members?) What criteria are you using to identify noncore functions?

2. How will you manage a network of outsourced personnel?

Envision how you will manage the relationships to achieve your quality goals and to ensure you are not diverting too much time from managing the core functions of the association.

Potential Shifts

▼ FROM	▼ TO
Outsourcing to reduce costs	Outsourcing for strategic advantages (creating value and leveraging resources)
Staff do everything	Staff concentrate on what they do best
More staff are needed to provide more services	Liberate staff time through outsourcing and technology usage

Competition and Alliances

▶ *An increasing vulnerability to competition will require associations to become more vigilant about new types of competitors and to seek out nontraditional allies.*

The Findings

- **Associations are more vulnerable than ever to competition.**
Thanks to information technology and the Internet, your members are easily accessible to your competitors. Conversely, this same technology gives your members the mobility to seek out other sources of information and services (which, when coupled with their rising expectations, creates a potent combination). Plus, a greater diversity within your membership means there are more niche markets for others to target.

In another ASAE Foundation survey, three out of four respondents (76%) indicated they were facing increasing competition. Most frequently, they cited these sources of competition:

- Another association (either a specialty association or one formed by mergers): 83%
- Another service provider: 58%
- Another publisher: 17%
- For-profit trade show: 16%
- Other source: 20%

- **Increased competition is coming from unexpected sources.**
The competitive landscape is shifting rapidly for associations. For example, increased competition for the adult education market seems to be coming from corporate training programs—employee education is the fastest growing learning segment in our society—while many trade shows are suffering declining attendance.

The panelists observed that their competitors are coming from unexpected places, including both nonprofit and for-profit organizations, in the areas of publications, trade shows, education, meetings, and Web-based services. Associations can no longer assume that they will face the same set of competitors year in and year out.

As an example, the Cambridge Information Network is a private sector community for information technology executives. Cambridge Technology Partners, a consulting firm, used its expertise to create the network for high-level, peer-to-peer interaction. Membership in the online community is free, with several association-like features (e.g., meetings and publications) included for a fee. By all outward appearances, the network appears to be a credible form of competition to the traditional association model.

- **Alliances with nontraditional partners.** As a consequence of increased competition, associations are more actively seeking alliances with nontraditional partners as well as with old competitors.

For example, Amazon.com, the virtual super-bookstore, is working with associations and other organizations to create online bookstores of interest to their constituencies. Through the Amazon Associates program, associations can customize book collections, publish reviews, and help readers purchase the books through a link to Amazon.com. As another example, Microsoft has built alliances with ASAE and the U.S. Chamber of Commerce to reach the small business market.

- **"Supercharged" alliances to gain core competencies and extend markets.** Moving beyond nontraditional partnerships, some associations are looking to alliances that are considered "supercharged" because they:

  - Deliver new competencies to the organization.
  - Attract partners willing to invest in the association's efforts.
  - Open up access to new markets and new distribution channels.
  - Lend significant credibility to the association's image in areas such as public policy, education, certification, and consumer awareness.

As associations enter into nontraditional alliances, they will need to rethink various facets of their corporate relationships. For example, they may need to shift from an "affinity program mindset" (offering discount programs as a convenience to members) to a "value creation mindset" (working with outside partners to add more value to the information or resources already possessed by the association).

Another potential shift is away from a "mailing list mindset" (trading on the value of your membership database) to a "marketing consultant mindset" (actively working with partners to help them customize products and services specifically targeted to your members).

Discussion and Exploration

1. What is your association doing to spot emerging competition?

- What are your members buying? From whom?

- Where else are they participating and giving their time?

- Who else is collecting information about your members?

2. What are you doing to seek new forms of partnerships and alliances?

Are you seeking out new partners and alliances in order to:

- Make new and highly desirable services available to your members?

- Deliver your products and services to new customers?

- Help your staff gain new skills and expertise?

- Gain investments to help your association extend itself into new markets?

Potential Shifts

▼ FROM	▼ TO
Few competitors/monopolistic environment	Highly competitive environment
Currently a competitor	Our next partner
Association's franchise with members acts as barrier to potential competitors	Entry of competitors from unexpected sources
Affinity program partners	Nontraditional and supercharged alliances

Consolidation and Mergers

▶ *As consolidation and mergers occur with greater speed and unpredictability, associations must become more proactive in dealing with the resulting chain reaction, which affects revenues, services, and membership categories.*

The Findings

The consolidation and mergers occurring among their memberships greatly affect associations' anticipated revenues, scheduled services, and existing membership categories. Many expect to face a shakeout as consolidation and downsizing affects their members. This, in turn, is putting pressure on certain associations to consolidate or merge with other associations.

- **Consolidation and mergers are occurring at an unexpected speed.** Often there are few warning signs: Major consolidations can sweep through an industry in a matter of months or a year. The often unpredictable nature of this trend makes ongoing environmental scanning essential as an "early warning system."

- **Associations need to adopt a proactive posture.** The speed at which this trend can unfold means that an association must begin planning before, not after, consolidations and mergers take hold. The use of scenario planning and asking "what if" questions will become more common as associations learn to anticipate the consequences of this trend and develop contingency plans.

  Scenarios are especially helpful in examining how membership categories would be realigned after consolidations, including the effect of such realignments on the association's revenue stream. In some industries, only the large or medium-sized businesses are surviving. In others, the gap is widening between the large and small members; the needs of each group may become too diverse for one association to satisfy.

  The panelists expressed a new willingness to seek mergers with other associations. Here are two questions to ask whenever an industry or profession is represented by multiple associations:

  - What audience is being represented by all participating associations? How much do we overlap? Will the overlaps eventually diminish the association's value?

  - What's the purpose of our organization in relation to the other associations in the industry or profession? What are the advantages for combining missions and visions?

Discussion and Exploration

1. What are you doing to scan your members' business environment to anticipate the possibility of consolidations and mergers that may occur in the next five years?

2. Where else can you obtain information about your members' changing business environment?

3. Develop "what if" scenarios to envision how this trend might affect your membership and your association.

Potential Shifts

▼ FROM	▼ TO
Reactive stance and backpedaling due to budget shortfalls	Contingency plans that anticipate consolidations and mergers
Fear of losing the traditional membership base	Boldly seeking and creating new opportunities as realignments occur

Globalization

▶ *As their members become less bound by geography, time zones, culture, and language in their business and professional relationships, associations will have to redefine their own boundaries accordingly.*

The Findings

- **Associations, and the members they serve, are boundary-less.**
  The economies of nations are becoming increasingly interconnected, and the effect of that is felt among associations' memberships. Competition and new opportunities are as likely to come from across the globe as down the street.

    Powerful economic, technological, political, and social forces drive globalization. These forces include revolutionary advances in communications and computing (e.g., the Internet), the size and integration of capital markets, deregulation of industries, and the building of democratic institutions around the world.

  - International members are increasingly interested in and able to seek out U.S. associations in their search for knowledge.

  - Any association, regardless of size and location, should consider itself capable of serving international members.

  - Domestic members are looking to their associations for information and guidance on how to participate in the global economy. Members also want their associations to advance the profession's or trade's ability to operate across borders.

    "Going international" can be as simple as meeting with your association's counterparts outside the United States every two years or establishing overseas chapters. Or, you might consider creating specific products to serve your international members, revising your governance structure to encourage international representation on the board, and expanding educational programs to reach groups outside the United States.

Discussion and Exploration

Associations seeking to evaluate their international opportunities are strongly advised to make use of the *ASAE Global Opportunities* online service, developed by the ASAE International Section to help members evaluate, understand, and manage an association's transition to the global marketplace. This service is available through ASAE's Web site at http://www.asaenet.org. There you can find a comprehensive "International Self-Assessment Audit" to begin the evaluation process.

Potential Shifts

▼ FROM	▼ TO
U.S.-focused association with some international members	**Truly international organization with a global mindset and culture**
Limited by geographical boundaries, culture, or language	**Using technology to create a worldwide network and instant communication**

Image Building

▶ *Increasing public scrutiny and
competition will lead associations
(professional and philanthropic
organizations, as well as trades) to
defend their members' credibility
and to promote the unique value
of their services or activities.*

The Findings

An increasingly competitive environment is driving members to look to their associations for help in establishing the unique value of their services or activities. This is occurring not only in trade associations but also in professional and philanthropic organizations. Furthermore, increased public and government scrutiny is fueling increased activity in such areas as setting standards and establishing professional credentials/accreditation programs; defending members in the face of negative public opinion; and promoting responsible (ethical) member behavior.

Associations must evaluate their credibility with the general public, members, nonmembers, and government (both regulators and legislators). This trend will place a demand on associations for:

- **Continuous tracking of constituents' perceptions.** In today's volatile environment, constituent perceptions can shift rapidly, often in a matter of weeks or days. The tracking of constituent awareness and perception cannot be a haphazard or occasional affair (e.g., attitude surveys once every 10 years). It must become a more frequent, ongoing event.

- **Greater sophistication and quality in image building.** Because the stakes are higher—and constituents often more difficult to influence— associations will need to continually improve the quality and sophistication of their outreach efforts if they wish to achieve success. Attention must be paid to state-of-the-art techniques used by public relations professionals in areas such as public opinion research, strategic goal setting, and the use of technology to deliver messages and build coalitions.

- **Greater accountability for outcomes.** Members will come to expect tangible benefits and measurable results for the dollars they invest in their associations' outreach efforts. Image building campaigns will be judged less by the "glitz factor" and more by defensible research that shows a measurable improvement in public opinion or an increased influence on purchasing decisions.

- **Investment decisions.** In some cases, the resources required to conduct highly effective outreach programs may exceed an association's capacity. This will require them to carefully evaluate the cost/benefit ratio of investing in public outreach versus other program areas that might be more essential to their mission statement.

Discussion and Exploration

1. How are you determining which audiences and messages are strategically important for the future of your mission?

2. How are you benchmarking your image with these audiences?

3. How are you communicating the results of your efforts back to your members?

Potential Shifts

▼ FROM	▼ TO
Image building an issue primarily for trades	Image building an issue primarily for trades, professional, and philanthropic organizations
Narrow focus on lobbying or public policy	Broad focus including public policy, public education, and coalition building
Association's job to promote members' products or services	Members and association collaborate to build customer/client relationships

CHAPTER

Association Characteristics

*Influence the perceptions of your volunteer leadership,
staff, and members as they chart the organization's
future direction and velocity.*

H ow many times has your association begun to design something new
and visionary only to be reigned in by traditional thinking and mindsets?
The gravitational pull of current practices and processes can be very
strong and often unconscious.

In the process of conducting the 1998 Environmental Scan, we
learned that stereotyping associations by size and type presents just such
a barrier to future thinking. When designing the environmental scan, we
postulated that different trends and their consequences would emerge
based on the size and type of the organization. For example, we expected
one set of trends for small individual membership organizations and
another set of trends for large trade associations. We learned, however,
that the same broad set of trends seems to affect all associations, regardless of their size (small, medium, or large), type (trade or individual
membership organization), or location (Los Angeles, Chicago, or
Washington, D.C.).

The effects of these trends can be best seen and understood by board
and staff when examined through five association characteristics. When
an association is oblivious to its characteristics, leadership's ability to
envision the future will be constrained. The characteristics are:

- Organizational culture
- The business, profession, or cause being served
- Life stage of the association
- Organizational resources
- Members' career development and life stage

Before boards and staff can engage in a dialogue about the future,
there must be a common understanding or foundation for interpreting the
trends. For example, what if different cultures exist among a board and its
staff? Each group's interpretations of the same trends will diverge in significant ways. Likewise, a discussion about trends will diverge if different
members of a board do not have the same viewpoint about the business or
profession served by the association—or if staff members don't agree
about the nature of the association's resources.

For this reason, an assessment and discussion of the five characteristics will be highly useful before embarking upon a dialogue about the
future. Analyzing the characteristics and their importance, arriving at
areas of common understanding, and identifying areas where viewpoints
diverge will greatly enhance your ability to facilitate a rich and robust
dialogue.

On the following pages, you'll find a detailed explanation of each characteristic, as well as exploratory exercises and sample dialogue exercises.

Organizational Culture

An association is defined by and demonstrates those values and perceptions embodied by its leaders, staff, members, and customers. The shared values within that shared culture shape the organization's ability to influence anything. Stated another way, the volunteer leaders, staff, and members are the association's "cultural ambassadors."

A report compiled by the Task Force on Innovation, Change and Leadership of the ASAE Executive Management Section recommends the need to create an association culture that is "change friendly." This entails moving from the traditional *command-and-control (risk reluctant)* model to one that is *collaborative (risk exploratory)*. The report strongly suggests investigating your organization's culture to provide a deeper understanding of what is needed to secure a positive change environment.

What type of culture does the future demand of your association?

What would exemplify a collaboration/risk exploratory culture?

- Establishing supercharged strategic alliances and pursuing opportunities

- Exploring new financial approaches to deploy expeditionary products and services

- Focusing attention on emerging member needs and outcomes

- Empowering volunteers and staff with a push for a shared vision

- Offering professional development opportunities to staff

- Increasing diversity (ideological, demographic, etc.)

What aspects of your culture are holding you back?

What typifies the *command-and-control/risk-reluctant* culture?

- Better to miss an opportunity than to make a mistake
- A "not-on-my-watch" attitude of stewardship
- Focus on sustaining a process
- Generational conflicts for power and influence
- Improving "efficiency" as the single means to change

In discussing organizational culture, scan panelists described how an organization's shared values tend to persist over time through changes in the membership's composition. They become entrenched in the association's communications, event designs, product offerings, and decision-making processes, thus establishing specific behavior patterns that new members, leaders, and staff are automatically assumed to know and agree to follow.

Identifying your organizational behaviors, especially where they restrict the perception of future opportunities, is critical. To uncover these assumptions requires conversations with all parties involved in the organization—volunteer leadership, staff, members, and customers.

Sample Dialogue Exercise

In *The Organizational Unconscious*, Robert F. Allen cites several areas to assess when exploring one's culture and its corresponding behaviors. Use the list below to engage volunteer leaders and staff in unearthing your organization's culture and values. At times, the exercise may seem like a historical journey—back to the reasons why "this is the way we do things around here." Use the resulting insights to realign your culture and leverage your future relevance.

What behaviors and actions represent your organizational culture?

- Leadership—What gets confronted? What gets avoided?

- Modeling behavior—Who are the leadership models? How do they reflect your future?

- Commitment to change and exploration—How demonstrated? Where demonstrated? By whom?

- Innovation and development—How does it happen? Who participates? What is measured?

- Communication—What knowledge is shared? With whom? What hoarded? From whom?

- Interactivity—What kinds are encouraged? Where occurring? Who included?

- Rewards and recognition—What are the rewards? What gets positive reinforcement? Negative?

- Resource allocation—What is the money spent on? Where is staff and volunteer time spent?

• Values and responsibilities—Any differences between what the volunteer leadership and staff believe in, practice, and use to guide them in their leadership? What will they need to meet the challenges of your future?

Provocative Questions

You can use the following sample questions to explore organizational culture and to provoke other questions during your association's ongoing leadership dialogues. There are no wrong answers to these questions—only opportunities to discover the underlying pitfalls, hurdles, obstacles, and hindrances, as well as the springboards, catapults, bridges, and innovations that will move your organization into the future.

1. What three adjectives would your board use to describe your organization? Your members? Your staff? Your customers?

    1. _____
    2. _____
    3. _____

    Do they agree? Do the descriptions complement one another? Are they aligned? If not, what do their differences imply?

2. What do your membership categories reflect? What images do they represent?
    ☐ Future audiences
    ☐ Past loyalties
    ☐ Current "groupies"
    ☐ A balanced mix

3. To what extent is your staff better at:
    ☐ creating original programs
    ☐ retooling existing programs
    ☐ collaborating with alliances
    ☐ copying the competition

4. Typically, an organization rewards what it values—for what do you recognize your volunteers and staff?
    ☐ contributing to body of knowledge
    ☐ governance expertise and longevity
    ☐ membership activities
    ☐ representational and coalition efforts
    ☐ fund-raising
    ☐ collaboration and innovation
    ☐ other _____

5. Do you have a shared set of cultural values that both the volunteer leadership and staff believe in, practice, and use to guide your association's work? What are they?

6. As the association plots its future course, what values are most essential to champion that vision?

The Business, Profession, or Cause Being Served

The 1990 Hudson Institute report, *The Value of Associations to American Society*, said: "Associations exist first to serve those interests of their members or their public constituencies not met sufficiently through individual action. Both associations composed of individuals and those composed of business firms serve the collective interests of their members and constituencies."

Association executives participating on the 1998 Environmental Scan Panels frequently challenged the continued relevance of associations. They were willing to ask the difficult questions: "Will associations exist in the future?" and "How does one remain relevant in the face of change?"

The consensus of the scan research was clear. Remaining relevant in an ever-changing world requires bold leadership, with both elected leaders and staff engaged in an ongoing dialogue with present and future organizational stakeholders. To prepare for the 21st century, you must continually question, "What purpose does our organization serve?" and "How is it relevant?"

Peter Drucker, in his workbook *The Five Most Important Questions You Will Ever Ask About Your Nonprofit Organization*, provides a user friendly guide for investigating an organization's present and future purpose. This assessment tool, which includes five main questions and 21 supporting inquiries, focuses on the values, goals, and expectations of an organization's future. Clarifying your organization's intention and purpose helps guide volunteers and staff as they process the trend information and evaluate its future relevancy. Here are some questions to ask:

- What do your members consider relevant and valuable? Your customers?

- Are you providing it in a useful and responsive manner?

- What makes your organization relevant in today's business environment? Education? Knowledge creation? Representation? What else?

- What are you trying to achieve? How are you measuring its success? Its failure?

- What is volatile in your industry's, profession's, or business environment to alter what you are trying to achieve?

- Whom do you currently serve? Are they pertinent as future members or customers?

- What will your members need in the future that they will expect you to provide? What is your association's potential for meeting those future expectations?

- What resource allocations are being made now to prepare? How are staffing competencies being adapted?

Sample Dialogue Exercise

Using the corporate examples of relevant value and the provocative questions listed below, engage your volunteer leaders and staff in exploring your organization's relevance and value as it relates to the industry, business, profession, or cause it serves.

Match the relevant value to its source. Create a statement to validate your organization:

1. Products and services when consumers want them	_____ A. Crayola Crayon
2. Respect for individual initiative	_____ B. Girl Scouts
3. People working more effectively	_____ C. FedEx
4. Fun and creative self-expression	_____ D. Merck & Co.
5. Self-confident and self-respecting young women	_____ E. 3M
6. Preserving and improving human life	_____ F. Steelcase
7. Responsiveness, on time with no excuses	_____ G. General Electric
8. Champion the champions	_____ H. Domino's Pizza
9. Boundary-less, speed and stretch	_____ I. General Mills

Your organization's validation statement: _____

(Answers appear on the next page)

Provocative Questions

- Are *members'* perceptions of your relevance and value different than that of your *customers'*?

- Has your organization outlived the value and relevance of its mission?

- Does the mission still herald the purpose of your organization and provide direction to volunteer leaders, members, and staff?

- Are your mission and purpose still compelling and reflective of your industry, profession, or cause?

- What stops the temptation of expanding into new sectors of activity that dilute the organization from its core competencies and are irrelevant to your future?

- Do you still have the power and influence to attract and retain members and customers?

- What boundaries must be crossed to remain relevant (international, cultural, generational, etc.)?

- What uniquely distinguishes you from your competitors? Relates you to your strategic alliances?

- Is the "reality of your relevance" a sufficient foundation upon which your association can build its future?

Quiz Answers: A-4, B-5, C-7, D-6, E-2, F-3, G-9, H-1, I-8.

Life Stage of the Association

In *A Child's Garden of Misinformation*, Art Linkletter writes, "The four stages of man are infancy, childhood, adolescence, and obsolescence." With a lot less humor and a lot more purpose, associations follow that same developmental path—but with a few more stages thrown in. If all goes well, they also experience *growth* and *maturity* before the predictable *decline* and *obsolescence* stages arrive.

Could an association remain ageless—never become obsolete? Remain forever relevant? The answer is yes! With leadership, vision, and the vigilance to manage and expand the organization's intellectual capital (its wisdom, knowledge, experiences, and insights), it *is* possible. Your organization is as vibrant, vital, and relevant as the knowledge you are sharing—that's the key to being an ageless organization.

Like their programs, services, and products, organizations have developmental stages and relevant cycles and certain resources required to sustain them. Rarely are "planned obsolescence strategies" on the agenda at board or staff meetings in regard to an organization's mission, vision, or product/program portfolio. As one scan panelist noted, "If we were starting an association from scratch, all of these trends would be easier to deal with."

Be on the lookout for signs of aging relevance. They occur when the organization:

- Becomes driven by process, not outcomes
- Looks inward for solutions, not outward
- Experiences decreased effectiveness in the face of change
- Uses most of the existing resources to maintain the status quo
- Witnesses little, if any, experimentation occurring
- Has more interest in maintaining "islands of knowledge" than expanding its sharing capacity

Remember: Your association is as old as its youngest visionary leader.

Sample Dialogue Exercise

- Is your association expending additional resources by delivering, in outmoded ways, programs and services with relevant content?

- Where and how is your association positioning itself to remain relevant with its programs, products, and experiences? Are you "over serving" a segment of your membership? Which audiences are you "under serving"?

- Is your association perpetuating a governance structure that resists change? Is "not on my watch" an appropriate strategy for keeping your organization relevant?

In *Successful Association Leadership,* Glenn Tecker and Marybeth Fidler address the cyclical nature of association development and the corresponding cycles of association initiatives, programs, and services. They note, "From the moment an organization is established, it must strive to secure its growth, its competitive positioning and the required resources to sustain its existence and future viability. As it develops and matures, more and more resources may be necessary to sustain its existence. Unless the organization is adept at staying contemporary, its position will erode and its existence will cease!"

Associations must consciously evaluate their life stage in relation to the validity of their mission as well as the validity of the products and services they offer. The relevance of your leadership selection process, your staff's roles and responsibilities, and the overall allocations of resources should also be evaluated.

Based on the results of the ASAE Foundation's *Trend Analysis Survey,* for example, many associations focus heavily on launching new programs without paying equal attention to retiring irrelevant ones. Consider this: 82% of the respondents indicated their associations will be initiating major new programs, while only 32% anticipated eliminating programs.

Provocative Questions

- Where does the organization focus its resources, energy, and momentum?
    - Generating new ideas and rolling out new programs to remain relevant?
    - Nurturing new leadership that represents the organization's future?
    - Realigning the focus of the organization to secure its ongoing relevance?
    - Maintaining old programs, processes, and structures to preserve the status quo?
    - Managing and expanding the organization's intellectual capital?
    - What challenges to your existing culture and systems (communications, governance, technology, etc.) are posed by the need for rapid development of future programs and services?

Organizational Resources

From conventional assets and traditional budgets, to external partnerships and collaborations, associations have begun to redefine and recalculate their resources. The explosion of the Internet and electronic commerce—plus the encroachment of for-profit enterprise into the association community—is forcing associations to question the old rules of allocating resources in favor of the new rules based on leveraging existing resources and making strategic investments.

The traditional funding/development model has limited responsiveness to member needs, venture opportunities, or staff insights. It operates from a finite planning horizon. The first step in the traditional model is to assess possible funding (budget availability). This is followed by an examination of what to fund.

The new model, however, requires both new sources of financial capital and the flexibility to move with speed when venturing through a "window of opportunity." The first step then becomes creating compelling needs, followed by the organization mobilizing to leverage existing funding and/or secure additional funding if needed. In other words, instead of allocating your resources, leverage and invest them.

In *Charting Assured Migration Paths to the Knowledge Age*, Donald Norris talks about extending association resources though the use of supercharging strategic alliances. He says, "Strategic alliances will become even more important as associations move into the Knowledge Age. These alliances will fulfill multiple functions. First, they provide expertise and a mechanism for acquiring basic competencies that are necessary to meet the needs of Knowledge Age customers. Second, these alliances will provide levels of resources—financial, technological, and process—necessary to create product development and learning infrastructure. Third, many of these strategic allies may provide customer bases to mitigate the risk of rolling out new generations of expeditionary products."

Sample Dialogue Exercise

- How have *resources* been defined and accumulated in the past? What succeeded? What failed?

- Do you view your budget as a constraint or an asset? Why?

- What are your current sources of capital for investments? Do you have compelling projects on the drawing board that will attract investments from entirely new sources?

- Who have been your traditional affinity partners?

- How could your association leverage these *nontraditional resources:*
    - Experience profile of your volunteer leadership? The general membership?
    - Expertise and competencies of your staff?
    - Your access to clout, influence, and power?
    - Technology providers?
    - Learning/educational providers?
    - Alliances of strategic investors?

- Consider the effect the following "resources" will have on your association's ability to generate expeditionary programs and projects:
    - The intellectual capital of your members and staff
    - The relationship reach of your members and staff
    - The accumulated "knowledge portfolio" of your organization

      – The multi-functional alliances outside your specific association
        community

Provocative Questions

- How are you partnering with technology companies to leverage your resources?

- What strategic alliances with past competitors (for-profit and non-profit) would best serve your members in the future? Your customers? Your stakeholders?

- How could your association capitalize on its ability to generate influence?

- Which strategic nonfinancial alliance would create exposure for your association in areas where you aren't represented but should be in the future? With audiences you don't have but want in the future?

- What is the "street value" of your brand identity? Your knowledge portfolio?

- Where will you leverage your knowledge portfolio for the greatest return?

- How is your organization nurturing and expanding its intellectual capital?

Members' Career Development and Life Stage

Associations have routinely profiled and segmented their membership when analyzing programs and services. Depending on its members' generational groupings; their length of membership; their years in the profession, business, or industry; and job titles, an association could confidently build its portfolio of programs, products, and member services.

Traditionally, educational programs were planned and promoted, volunteer roles created (though not always filled), committees formed, resources and responsibilities assigned, and communication messages crafted to fit the association's various segments. Such traditional membership profiling, however, is becoming irrelevant. With life expectancies increasing, generational variances driving choices, and career-switching becoming the norm, most associations' programs and communications have not kept up with the subtle distinctions that mark different career and life-stage preferences.

For instance, as the scan panelists noted, the correlation between a member's participation in or loyalty to the association and his or her age or years of membership is not automatic. Associations will have to adjust their leadership structures, educational offerings, volunteer opportunities, and networking experiences to their changing membership's needs and expectations.

Life's "human arithmetic" used to be simpler: one employer for a life time, one marriage, having children, and so forth. Today, many first-time brides are over 30 and first-time mothers over 40, single-father households are increasing in number, older people in second marriages are having children, and empty-nesters are becoming parental care-givers. Americans are refusing to be bound by traditional demographic profile descriptors.

Do the arithmetic for your membership:

Traditional career "stages"	Cumulative career experiences (management, finance, marketing, sales, project development, etc.)	Total years in the industry, business, or profession of association	Total years in the association
Novice/Rookie			
Intermediate			
Advanced/Seasoned			
Mature/Veteran			
Master/Elder			

Sample Dialogue Exercise

- Members in your organization and new participants to your industry, business, or profession have amassed a variety of career experiences valuable and desirable to the association. How will you learn who they are? What they know? Marshall them as resources?

- Their competencies were developed by the corporate arena, government/military service, volunteer leadership in previous career opportunities, and even from other segments of the nonprofit community. How will this influx of new expertise and perspective alter your association?

- Doctors, dentists, and architects have a lifetime career track with progressive certification. Are there any similarities within your association to these models?

Based on statistics presented in *Managing Your Future as an Association* (Coates and Jarrett), it is clear that Baby Boomers are likely to stay in the workforce longer then the age group before them. They'll accumulate more experiences and more education along the way. Diversity in cultural backgrounds, ages, religions, and race will also influence your organization. Just consider that 12% of the workers in U.S. corporations in 1995 were minorities, compared with 2% in 1966. A diverse workforce brings different experiences and perceptions into the workplace mix.

From Generation X members will come increased expectations for seamless communication and perpetual learning through technology, plus the advantages derived from diversity relationships. Accumulated life experiences and acquired competencies will become levelers on the "participation/involvement playing field." As a result, an organization must value life experience as well as association experience.

Newly arriving members may appear to be novices to your industry or profession when actually they are at a "new plateau" in their current career. Take care not to de-value, disregard, or underestimate what they have accomplished. Associations must find ways to accommodate all members according to their career and life experiences when creating participation/involvement opportunities. For example: Younger "new" members may have more expertise with technology than most of your existing volunteer leadership, allowing them to "mentor" less experienced (but perhaps older) members.

Provocative Questions

- Who is joining your association? Who is entering your association's industry, business, or professional arena? How similar are they to the current member profile? How different?

- Is your association altering its recruitment and retention offerings to accommodate membership/experience shifts?

- What volunteer opportunities will your organization offer to capitalize on its diverse membership expertise and experience?

- What are the career stages of your staff?

- How will this information on "member experiences" be captured?

Bibliography

Abrahams, Jeffrey. *The mission statement book: 301 corporate mission statements from America's top companies.* Berkeley, Calif.: Ten Speed Press, 1995.

Allen, Robert F., Certner Barry Judd, and Charlotte Kraft. *The organizational unconscious, how to create the corporate culture you want and need.* Morristown, N.J.: Human Resources Institute, 1987.

American Society of Association Executives Executive Management Section Council. *Core competencies for association executives.* Washington, D.C.: American Society of Association Executives Executive Management Section Council, 1998. (Unpublished.)

American Society of Association Executives Foundation. *Grant research.* Washington, D.C.: American Society of Association Executives Foundation, 1990. (Unpublished.)

———. *The value of associations to American society: A report by the Hudson Institute.* Washington, D.C.: American Society of Association Executives Foundation, 1990. (Out of print.)

Barrett, Richard. *Liberating the corporate soul, building a visionary organization.* Boston: Butterworth Heinemann, 1998.

Burrus, Daniel. *Techno trends: 24 technologies that will revolutionize our lives.* New York: Harper Business, 1993.

Coates, Joseph, and Jennifer Jarratt. *Managing your future as an association: Thinking about trends and working with their consequences.* Washington, D.C.: American Society of Association Executives Foundation, 1994.

Drucker Foundation. *The community of the future.* San Francisco: Jossey-Bass, 1998.

———. *The leader of the future.* San Francisco: Jossey-Bass, 1996.

———. *The organization of the future.* San Francisco: Jossey-Bass, 1997.

Drucker, Peter F. *The five most important questions you will ever ask about your nonprofit organization.* San Francisco: Jossey-Bass, 1993.

Ernstthal, Henry L., and Bob Jones IV. *Principles of association management,* third edition. Washington, D.C.: American Society of Association Executives, 1996.

Fahey, Liam, and Robert M. Randall. *Learning from the future: Competitive foresight scenarios.* New York: John Wiley & Sons, Inc., 1998.

Hamel, Gary, and C. K. Prahalad. *Competing for the future.* Boston: Harvard Business School Press, 1994.

Jarratt, Jennifer. *Managing your future as an association: Thinking about trends and working with their consequences 1997-2020.* Washington, D.C.: American Society of Association Executives Foundation, 1997.

Lipman-Blumen, Jean. *Connective edge: Leading in an interdependent world.* San Francisco: Jossey-Bass, 1996.

Norris, Donald M. *Charting assured migration paths to the knowledge age.* Washington, D.C.: American Society of Association Executives, 1997.

Norris, Donald M. *Thriving in the knowledge age.* Washington, D.C.: American Society of Association Executives, 1997.

———. *Transforming higher education: A vision for learning in the 21st century.* Ann Arbor, Mich.: Society for College and University Planning, 1995.

———. *Market-driven management: Lessons learned from 20 successful associations.* Washington, D.C.: American Society of Association Executives, 1990.

Peppers, Don, and Martha Rogers. *Enterprise one-to-one.* New York: Currency Doubleday, 1997.

———. *The one to one future: Building relationships one customer at a time.* New York: Currency Doubleday, 1993.

Peters, Tom. *The circle of innovation: You can't shrink your way to greatness.* New York: Alfred Knopf, 1997.

———. *The pursuit of WOW: Every person's guide to topsey-turvey times.* New York: Vintage Books, 1994.

Popcorn, Faith. *The Faith Popcorn report on the future of your company, your world and your life.* New York: Harper Business, 1992.

Schwartz, Peter. *The art of the long view: Planning for the future in an uncertain world.* New York: Currency Doubleday, 1995.

Senge, Peter M. *The fifth discipline fieldbook.* New York: Currency Doubleday, 1994.

———. *The fifth discipline: The art & practices of the learning organization.* New York: Currency Doubleday, 1994.

Smith, J. Walker, and Ann Clurman. *Rocking the ages: The Yankelovich report on generational marketing.* New York: Harper Business, 1997.

Snyder, David Pearce, and Gregg Edwards. *Future focus: An association executive's guide to a decade of change and choice.* Washington, D.C.: American Society of Association Executives Foundation, 1984.

Steckel, Richard. *Filthy rich & other nonprofit fantasies: Changing the way nonprofits do business in the 90's.* Berkeley, Calif.: Ten Speed Press, 1988.

Tecker, Glenn, and Marybeth Fidler. *Successful association leadership: Dimensions of 21st-century competency for the CEO.* Washington, D.C.: American Society of Association Executives Foundation, 1993.

Tecker, Glenn, Kermit Eide, and Jean Frankel. *Building a knowledge-based culture—Using 21st century decision-making in associations.* Washington, D.C.: American Society of Association Executives Foundation, 1997.

van der Heijden, Kees. *Scenarios: The art of strategic conversation.* New York: John Wiley & Sons, 1996.

Suggested Reading

Albrecht, Karl, and Ron Zemke. *Service America! Doing business in the new economy.* Homewood, Ill.: Warner Books, 1985.

Baden, Clifford. *Adult learning in associations: Models for good practice.* Washington, D.C.: American Society of Association Executives Foundation, 1997.

Bennis, Warren, and Joan Goldsmith. *Learning to lead: A workbook on becoming a leader.* Reading, Mass.: Addison-Wesley, 1997.

Bennis, Warren, and Michael Mische. *The 21st century organization: Reinventing through reengineering.* San Francisco: Jossey-Bass, 1995.

Butler, Wilford A. *Attracting, organizing and keeping members.* Washington, D.C.: American Society of Association Executives, 1989.

King, Larry. *Future talk: Conversations about tomorrow.* New York: Harper Collings, 1998.

Lee, Hugh, and Donald Dea. *World class Web sites.* Washington, D.C.: American Society of Association Executives Foundation, 1998.

Norris, Donald M. *Getting your association hooked on quality: A how-to guide and workbook for CEOs, volunteers and staff.* Washington, D.C.: American Society of Association Executives Foundation, 1999.

Sirkin, Arlene F., and Michael P. McDermott. *Keeping members—The myths & realities, CEO strategies for the 21st century success.* Washington, D.C.: American Society of Association Executives Foundation, 1995.

Appendix A
Environmental Scan Participants

The ASAE Foundation thanks the following for participating on the environmental scan trend analysis panels in Washington, D.C., Chicago, and Los Angeles.

Large Professional Association Trend Analysis Panel, Washington, D.C.

Suzanne R. Bliss, associate executive director, Juvenile Diabetes Foundation International, New York

Christine E. Burke, CAE, director of development, American Institute of Chemical Engineers Foundation, New York

John B. Cox, CAE, executive director, American Association of Pharmaceutical Scientists, Alexandria, Va.

Thomas C. Dolan, Ph.D., FACHE, CAE, president/CEO, American College of Healthcare Executives, Chicago

Harriet L. Fader, M.A., CAE, executive director, Diabetes Association of Greater Cleveland, Cleveland, Ohio

Robert A. Floyd, CAE, president, Texas Society of Association Executives, Austin, Texas

Paul J. Greeley, Jr. CAE, president, American Chamber of Commerce Executives, Alexandria, Va.

Judith C. Marden, Foundation director, Financial Women International, Arlington, Va.

Jeffrey D. Morgan, CAE, senior vice president, National Association of Professional Insurance Agents, Alexandria, Va.

Judy T. Neel, CAE, executive director, American Society of Safety Engineers, Des Plaines, Ill.

Bruce A. Ramirez, deputy executive director, Council for Exceptional Children, Reston, Va.

Sarah J. Sanford, CEO, American Association of Critical-Care Nurses, Aliso Viejo, Calif.

Thomas R. Schedler, CAE, executive director, American College of Foot and Ankle Surgeons, Park Ridge, Ill.

Cynthia Sheridan, CAE, associate director, Bank Marketing Association, Washington, D.C.

Lee VanBremen, Ph.D., CAE, executive vice president, College of American Pathologists, Northfield, Ill.

Pamela C. Williams, CAE, director of member services, Teachers of English to Speakers of Other Languages, Alexandria, Va.

Todd Wurschmidt, Ph.D., CAE, executive director, Ohio Association of Chiefs of Police, Inc., Dublin, Ohio

Large Trade Association Trend Analysis Panel, Washington, D.C.

Anne L. DeCicco, ECAM, CAE, president, Luggage & Leather Goods Manufacturers of America, New York

Warren Lasko, CEO, International Mortgage Bankers Association of America, Washington, D.C.

Donald B. Shea, president, Rubber Manufacturers Association, Washington, D.C.

John F. Sturm, president and CEO, Newspaper Association of America, Vienna, Va.

C. Richard Titus, executive vice president, Kitchen Cabinet Manufacturers Association, Reston, Va.

Small Trade and Professional Associations Trend Analysis Panel, Los Angeles

Sheryl Chalupa, executive director, Girl Scouts – Joshua Tree Council, Bakersfield, Calif.

Karen Conlon, president, California Association of Community Managers, Irvine, Calif.

June Davidson, president, American Seminar Leaders Association, Pasadena, Calif.

Mark W. Gilmore, executive vice president, Tri-Counties Association of Realtors, Walnut, Calif.

Kathy Hartman, executive vice president, Burbank Association of Realtors, Burbank, Calif.

Mary Ellen Hughes, CAE, executive director, Apartment Association of San Fernando Valley & Ventura County, Van Nuys, Calif.

Alberta E. Hultman, CAE, executive director, California Jewelers Association, Los Angeles

Susan E. Lovelace, executive director, San Diego County Dental Society, San Diego, Calif.

Colleen H. Richardson, CAE, executive director, California Thoracic Society, Tustin, Calif.

Frank L. Williams, executive officer, Building Industry Association Southern California – Baldy View, Rancho Cucamonga, Calif.

Medium Trade and Professional Associations Trend Analysis Panel, Los Angeles

James Gorman, executive vice president, California Motor Car Dealers Association, Playa Del Rey, Calif.

Danna L. McDonough, CAE, executive director, Los Angeles City Employees Association, Los Angeles

John W. Pearson, CEO, Christian Management Association, Diamond Bar, Calif.

Mary Riemersma, CAE, executive director, California Association of Marriage and Family Therapists, San Diego, Calif.

Ronald J. Surace, COO, American Industrial Real Estate Association, Los Angeles

Medium Trade and Professional Associations Trend Analysis Panel, Chicago

James J. Balija, CAE, executive director, American Association of Diabetes Educators, Chicago

Dennis Bozzi, president, Life Services Network of Illinois, Hinsdale, Ill.

Gary Clayton, CAE, executive vice president, Illinois Association of Realtors, Springfield, Ill.

Bonnie A. Cobean, CAE, executive vice president, Real Estate Brokerage Managers Council, Chicago

Alice DeForest, CAE, executive director, American Academy of Periodontology, Chicago

Darcy A. Dougherty RCE, CAE, CEO, Chicago Association of Realtors, Chicago

Ronald A. Henrichs, CAE, executive director, American Academy of Physical Medicine and Rehabilitation, Chicago

Robert L. Holding, president, Association of Home Appliance Manufacturers, Chicago

Charles D. Hughes, Jr., interim executive director, Illinois Community Action Association, Springfield, Ill.

Joseph R. McLennan, president, Management Association of Illinois, Broadview, Ill.

Daniel N. Myers, executive vice president and general manager, National Propane Gas Association, Lisle, Ill.

John A. Venator, executive vice president/CEO, Computing Technology Industry Association, Lombard, Ill.

Small Trade and Professional Associations Trend Analysis Panel, Chicago

Janet B. Bray, CAE, executive vice president, National Association of Enrolled Agents, Gaithersburg, Md.

Mary S. Feeley, executive director, Illinois Podiatric Medical Association, Chicago

Susan Fox, executive director, Society of American Archivists, Chicago

Robin B. Gray, Jr., executive vice president, National Electronic Distributors Association, Alpharetta, Ga.

Nona Wolfram Koivula, executive director, All America Selections, Downers Grove, Ill.

Robin Kriegel, CAE, executive director, American Association of Medical Society Executives, Chicago

Stephen L. Lamb, CAE, executive vice president, Mechanical Contractors Association, Chicago

George L. Patt, CAE, executive vice president, South Southwest Association of Realtors, Palos Heights, Ill.

Terese Penza, RCE, CAE, president and COO, North Shore Board of Realtors, Northbrook, Ill.

J. Vincent Shuck, executive director, American Academy of Implant Dentistry, Chicago

Reneta Webb, Ph.D., CAE, president, Partners in Learning, Chicago

William Wheeler, Jr. CAE, executive vice president, Chicago Association of Life Underwriters, Chicago

Hospitality Executives Trend Analysis Panel, Washington, D.C.

James Guy Bagg, director national accounts, Doral Golf Resort and Spa, Miami, Fla.

Warren J. Breaux, vice president of marketing, Opryland Hotel Convention Center, Nashville, Tenn.

David R. Evans, vice president and industry relations center, Starwood Hotels and Resorts Worldwide, Hotel Group, Seattle, Wash.

Richard B. Green, executive director association sales, Marriott Hotels and Resorts Mayflower Hotel, Washington, D.C.

Beverly W. Kinkade, CMP, CHME, vice president association sales, Starwood Hotels and Resorts Worldwide, Inc., Ballwin, Mich.

John F. Metcalfe, president, Associated Luxury Hotels Inc., Washington, D.C.

Phillip Mogle, regional director, Marriott Hotels and Resorts – National Accounts Office, McLean, Va.

Charles M. Robinson, director sales and promotion, Starwood Hotels and Resorts – Sales Office, Washington, D.C.

Peg Scherbarth, regional director of sales, Walt Disney Attractions Inc., Washington, D.C.

David Scypinski, director of convention marketing, Hilton Sales Worldwide, Washington, D.C.

Ellen D. Terry, director of sales, Ritz-Carlton Hotel Company – International Sales, Washington, D.C.

Convention and Visitors Bureau Executives Trend Analysis Panel, Washington, D.C.

Paul D. Astleford, president and CEO, Chicago Convention and Tourism Bureau, Chicago

Bruce Dozier, manager, Las Vegas Convention and Visitors Authority, Las Vegas

John A. Marks, president, San Francisco Convention and Visitors Bureau, San Francisco

Daniel E. Mobley, CAE, president, Washington D.C. Convention and Visitors Association, Washington, D.C.

Edward Nielsen, president and CEO, International Association of Convention and Visitors Bureaus, Washington, D.C.

William C. Peeper, executive director and CEO, Orlando Orange County Convention and Visitors Bureau, Orlando, Fla.

Christine Shimasaki, vice president sales and marketing convention center, San Diego Convention and Visitors Bureau, San Diego, Calif.

Kristine M. Sweeney, regional director of sales, New York Convention and Visitors Bureau, New York

Consultants Trend Analysis Panel, Washington, D.C.

Bruce Butterfield, CAE, president, The Forbes Group, Fairfax, Va.

James G. Dalton, CAE, president, Strategic Counsel, Derwood, Md.

Kathleen M. Krajewski, president, Krajewski and Associates Inc., Rockville, Md.

Georgia A. Patrick, president, The Communicators Inc., Jefferson, Md.

Annette E. Petrick, CAE, president, Petrick Outsourcing Unlimited Inc., Woodstock, Va.

Harmon O. Pritchard Jr., CAE, president, Pritchard Consulting Inc., Germantown, Md.

Arlene Farber Sirkin, president, Washington Resource Consulting Group Inc., Bethesda, Md.

Sheila Wexler, president, Wexler Marketing Group Inc., Alexandria, Va.

Special thanks go to the following for hosting the 1998 scan panels:

Amy L. Glad, executive vice president, Building Industry Association Southern California. Inc.,
Diamond Bar, Calif.

Pamela Hemann, CAE, Association Management Services, Pasadena, Calif.

The Law Offices of Jenner and Block, Washington, D.C.

J. C. Mahaffey, CAE, Association Forum of Chicagoland, Chicago

Appendix B
Instructions for Conducting a Future Scan Dialogue Session

Stories and narratives are proven and powerful methods for organizing information and dealing with complexity. Major corporations, such as 3M and Royal Dutch Shell, use storytelling and scenario techniques to analyze their changing environment, envision the future, and develop strategic and business plans.

Traditional techniques for understanding trends—such as forced ranking and cross-impact analysis grids—are valuable tools. By themselves, however, they do not sufficiently capture the full richness and implications of the future. Storytelling has a number of advantages:

- It is an intuitively comfortable approach for most people and therefore the easiest and most productive way to begin analyzing the trends.

- It presents findings in a real-world context rather than an artificial or purely theoretical one.

- Stories are memorable, making it easier for the board and staff to remember the essential points.

- Stories engage the board and staff by capturing their imagination and creating a sense of excitement about the future.

- Stories capture the four key elements necessary for understanding the trends. They define:
  - Relationships
  - Sequence of events
  - Cause and effect
  - Priority among items

If you would like to employ the storytelling approach to the future with your board and staff, here are the steps to take.

Preparing for a Session

Allocate at least three hours (more for larger groups) during a board or staff meeting. This technique works best with a minimum of 10 people and no more than 32 people.

Depending on the number of participants, divide them into subgroups of between five and eight people. The goal is to have at least two subgroups but no more than four. For each subgroup you will need the following materials:

- A flip chart
- Magic markers
- Two packages of 3M Post-It® notepads (3"×5" preferred).

Advance Reading Assignment

In advance of the futures discussion session, give all the participants a reading assignment: Ask them to read chapters 1 and 2.

Step 1: Debriefing — TIME: 30 to 40 minutes

Give participants the opportunity to review and discuss their reactions to the 14 trends by asking them to consider the three questions below. Discuss each question separately, and capture their responses on a flip chart.

- What was missing in the document? From your vantage point, are there important trends or changes that weren't covered?

- What are the biggest "a-has!" or insights you gained about the future? Are there "a-has" or insights you've gleaned from other sources? Name where (books, articles, Web sites) or who (in or out of the non-profit community).

- Is there anything in the document that made you say, "No way! I don't believe that will happen in the next two to five years"?

Step 2: What Will Be Different? — TIME: 30 minutes

Break into subgroups, each with five to eight people, and ask each group to create two lists. Instruct each group to divide their flipchart sheet in two columns: Mark the left-hand column *Different in the World* and the right-hand column *Different for the Association*.

Each group takes the next **20 minutes** to think about the trends and the discussion that just occurred. The participants should consider:

- What will be different in the next three to five years?
- What will be different in the world in terms of social, demographic, economic, technological, or political trends?
- What will be different for our association?

Each group then records its observations in the appropriately labeled column of the flip chart.

- In the left-hand column: Name the things that will be different in the world.
- In the right-hand column: Name the things that will be different for your association.

Note: Remind participants to work quickly and intuitively. They should concentrate on naming the issues. They do not have to explain or defend their choices.

Once they have completed their lists, each subgroup will review the results and take **10 minutes** to pick the *top three issues.* The top three issues should be marked with an asterisk.

Step 3: Create a Mini-Story — TIME: 30 to 40 minutes

Participants remain in their subgroups from the previous exercise to create a "mini-story" about the future. After completion, each subgroup will be responsible for telling its story to the entire panel. The story should take about a minute to tell.

As a starting point, each group creates a headline that describes the future. The mini-story flows from there, with each group given instructions to do the following:

- Look at the three trends the subgroup chose as being the most critical.

- Find ways these trends are interrelated (i.e., the story must demonstrate the relationship between the three trends).

- Reflect on the unique aspects of the association as revealed by the five association characteristics.

- Ensure the story takes place at least two years from now but no more than five years from today.

- Paint a scenario that is significantly different than today (i.e., it is surprising, unexpected, unanticipated).

- Make sure the story is plausible; it is based on facts and results from changes we know are occurring. While it may be surprising, the story is not meant to be fiction or fantasy.

Step 4: Reporting Out and Discussion — TIME: 60+ minutes

The entire group reconvenes. Each subgroup is allocated two minutes to name its top three issues and tell its mini-story (including the headline). **All the groups will report out before any discussion is allowed.**

After all the groups are done, the entire panel engages in a free-flowing discussion about what they have learned.

Here are some questions to guide the large group discussion:

- What do we agree on? What common themes or insights emerged in each of the mini-stories?

- Where do we diverge? What different themes or ideas emerged in one story but not the others? Why did those divergent themes emerge? What assumptions led the subgroups to interpret the future differently?

- What's missing? Stepping back and looking at all the stories, is there something missing that needs to be included or considered? What is it?

- What mega-opportunities for the association do the participants see in their mini-stories?

- What threats or issues of concern for the association do the participants see in their mini-stories?

- Which trends warrant further investigation or monitoring?

Thank You to Our Donors

It is with generous donations from the association community that the ASAE Foundation is able to conduct environmental scanning and fund future-directed research. We thank the following donors who have pledged contributions of $100,000 or more to the Foundation's Endowing the Future campaign:

American Airlines
CNA Insurance
Delta Air Lines
Hilton Hotels Corporation
Holiday Inn Worldwide
Hyatt Hotels Corporation
J.W. Marriott Foundation
Loews Hotels
Marriott Hotels Resorts & Suites
MBNA America
Northwest Airlines
Opryland Hotel Convention Center
Starwood Hotels & Resorts Worldwide, Inc.
United Airlines

Authors

The American Society of Association Executives (ASAE) Foundation commissioned two highly regarded consultants to the association community to produce this report.

Rhea L. Blanken founded Results Technology, Inc., Bethesda, Md., in 1982 to encourage and promote leadership, strategic thinking, and service within the association community. She has designed and conducted organizational retreats, workshops, and seminars for associations nationwide. Her clients have included the National Association of Homebuilders, Urban Land Institute, American Trucking Association, ASAE Foundation, National Food Processors Association, and American Water Resources Association.

Blanken is an ASAE Associate Fellow and a past chair of the ASAE Marketing Section. She has been a speaker at numerous ASAE annual meetings, section roundtables, and allied society meetings. She also has written several articles for ASAE section newsletters and has contributed to articles published in *Association Management* magazine.

She has a bachelor's of science degree in speech and communication from the University of North Carolina.

Allen Liff, of Ronin Marketing, Washington, D.C., is an independent consultant in the areas of strategic thinking and marketing for associations. He previously worked for the American Association of Museums, the American Institute of Architects, and the Independent Insurance Agents of America. He also has worked as a community organizer in low-income neighborhoods in Detroit, Mich., and Des Moines, Iowa.

Liff has made numerous presentations on strategic planning, including those made at the 1996 and 1997 ASAE Management and Technology conferences. He also has served as a member of the ASAE CEO Team. Liff has written several articles about strategic thinking and future issues for *Association Management* magazine.

Liff has a bachelor's of science degree in environmental engineering from Cornell University and a master's of public administration from George Washington University.